THE BOOK OF
MINIATURE
HORSES

THE BOOK OF
MINIATURE
HORSES

BUYING, BREEDING, TRAINING, SHOWING, AND ENJOYING

Written By
DONNA CAMPBELL SMITH

Photographs By
BRUCE CURTIS

THE LYONS PRESS
Guilford, Connecticut
An imprint of The Globe Pequot Press

DEDICATION

Jessica Dawn Smith, my granddaughter, knew long before I did that we had to have a Miniature Horse. Thank goodness she was able to convince me that was true. I dedicate this book to her.

The Lyons Press is an imprint of The Globe Pequot Press.

10 9 8 7 6 5 4 3 2 1

Printed in the United States of America

Designed by Sheryl P. Kober

Library of Congress Cataloging-in-Publication Data

Campbell, Donna, 1946–
    The book of miniature horses : buying, breeding, training, showing, and enjoying / Written by Donna Campbell Smith ; photographed by Bruce Curtis.
        p. cm.
    Includes bibliographical references.
    ISBN 1-59228-600-3 (trade cloth)
    1. Miniature horses. I. Title.
SF293.M56C36 2005
636.1'09—dc22

2005010356

TABLE OF CONTENTS

ACKNOWLEDGMENTS

There are many people who helped me write *The Book of Miniature Horses.* Leslie Ward, editor of *Young Rider* magazine, introduced me to Bruce Curtis. Bruce is an extraordinary photographer, who came up with the idea of a book about Miniature Horses and invited me to write the text. Thank you, Bruce and Leslie. I also thank Bruce for introducing me to his agent, Rita Rosenkranz. Rita, thank you for your hard work and good advice. Steven D. Price, who is the editor of this book, I thank you for your expertise and patience. Bless your heart.

Several Miniature Horse owners, trainers, and breeders and other experts shared their knowledge with me and I am thankful for their contributions. My friends and family who supported me by listening, smiling, and nodding politely while I talked about writing *The Book of Miniature Horses,* thank you. And last but not least, I thank my eldest daughter, Dineane. I would never have done it without her.

CHAPTER ONE

ORIGIN AND HISTORY OF THE MINIATURE HORSE

EOHIPPUS STOOD A MERE TEN TO TWELVE INCHES TALL AND walked the earth during the Pliocene period. The four-toed prehistoric horse, with its long head and roached back, bore little resemblance to today's smallest horse, the Miniature Horse, in spite of man's efforts to downsize it to prehistoric stature. Diminutive horses were found buried with Egyptian pharaohs, and during the Middle Ages they were popular pets for royal families. Legend tells us that King Henry VIII outlawed the ownership of small horses, and had all he could find slaughtered, but breeders managed to hide enough of the little horses to preserve the gene pool, and so today we have the Miniature Horse.

PIT PONIES

Coal was an important commodity far back in history. At first the fuel was mined from the ground's surface, but as human demand increased, men had to dig deeper and deeper. They used small horses to pull wagons of coal out of the tunnels; the smaller the horse, the easier the fit. Soon horses were being bred down to size for the express purpose of working in mines.

Coal miner with his pit pony.

It was the late 1800s before miniature—"midget" as they were called then—pit ponies were imported from Holland, Great Britain, and other European countries to the United States and Canada to replace women and children working in the mines. The soft coal mines of West Virginia, Virginia, and Kentucky had small tunnels that were only thirty-six inches high, so the ponies had to be smaller than thirty-four inches. The ponies worked hard, but reportedly were well cared for. Archie McIntyre writes in "Pit Pony—When Boys Mined Coal" that mining companies gave more consideration to the horses than to the men. "They had to buy the horses, but they got all the men they wanted for nothing."

McIntyre said the ponies had a strong sense of duty, stopping the minute the lights went out until the handler grasped their tail. The ponies then led them out of the dark. He wrote that many of the ponies he knew had been in the mines for over twenty years, never seeing the light of day; their stables were below ground inside the mines.

SMITH MCCOY

Walter Smith McCoy bred small pit ponies in West Virginia in the early 1900s. When machines began replacing the ponies, he discovered a new market for them. He was able to sell his smallest horses for better prices as novelty pets and exhibition animals, and he soon began to breed them smaller and smaller. His goal was to have horses that measured less than thirty-two inches. In the book *Moorman Field, Horse Trader*, Jacqueline and Thomas Field write that McCoy carried a walking stick with him whenever he went pony shopping. The stick had notches carved into it at thirty-two, thirty-four, and thirty-six inches, so he could measure ponies on the sly, without the owners knowing it. In a photo feature published by *Look* magazine in November 1965, McCoy said he could sell the "midget offspring" for $500 and up. He joked they were good lawn mowers and "ideal for four-year-olds who like to dangle their legs."

In the same article McCoy is said to have wagered $5,000 to $1,000 that no one could show him a smaller, full-grown, normal pony than his twenty-inch-tall horse named Sugardumpling. Pictures show Sugardumpling snacking in the kitchen and being walked on a leash by Mrs. McCoy like anyone's family dog.

Smith McCoy held the first Midget Pony Sale in Tazewell, Virginia.

With his herd numbering sixty at that writing, Smith McCoy is quoted as saying, "I know little about genes or genetics, but you can have crackpot good luck with ponies, just like people."

On September 16, 1967, McCoy held the first Midget Pony Sale in Tazewell, Virginia, to reduce his herd of one hundred horses to a more manageable fifty. He offered in a public ad $100 to anyone who could bring a pony that was smaller, while being "as good (not a dwarf)" as his midget ponies. People flocked to see and purchase his tiny horses, advertised as "the world's smallest midget ponies." McCoy urged people to come whether they wanted to buy or not, just to see his small and well-conformed ponies. Sales were on cash terms only.

Willis Parker

While McCoy is one of the best known early importers of tiny horses, *Life* magazine reported in its December 22, 1952, issue that Willis Parker, owner of a Hollywood animal agency, had four Miniature Horses brought from Sussex, England, to add to a collection of animals in miniature that were displayed at his Lilliput ranch in California. Parker, an animal trainer, provided animals for movies and television. Chauncey, Cedric, Ronnie, and the fourth horse (not named in the article) weighing in at an average of ninety pounds, joined the menagerie of small dogs, ducks, and miniature deer on Parker's farm as an oddity to amuse visitors.

Moorman Field

Another name well known to Miniature Horse breeders is Moorman Field of Bedford, Virginia. Field first raised the small equines to sell to mining companies as pit ponies. He and Smith McCoy became close friends through their pony dealings.

Moorman Field wanted a pony when he was a boy. He didn't get one then, and vowed when he had children of his own they would have ponies. They not only had ponies, but horses, mules, and various other exotic pets and fowl. However, Field is best known for his midget ponies. He began his Miniature Horse business first by raising Shetlands. He bought more land as his herd grew, and bred hundreds of Miniature Horses over his fifty-three-year career. It is probable that most of today's Miniature Horses could be traced to the Moorman Field "midget ponies" if pedigree records had been kept.

After he suffered a series of strokes Field held his first dispersal sale in the fall of 1961. The sale took place in Hollins, Virginia, with 250 head of horses offered for sale. In October 1962 another 250 horses were sold at auction, leaving the family with a mere 150 Miniature Horses. When Moorman Field died in 1965 his family continued the breeding of Miniature Horses for another twenty years.

JC WILLIAMS

JC Williams is another name synonymous with foundation Miniature Horses. He owned Dell Tera Miniature Horse Farm in Inman, South Carolina. The Dell Tera bloodlines are still sought after by breeders today, especially those who want to breed the smallest quality minis.

FALABELLA MINIATURE HORSES

A unique strain of the Miniature Horse is the Falabella. Its origin is South America and it has the longest history of any branch of Miniature Horses. It is believed that the first Falabellas were descendents of horses brought to South America in the sixteenth century by Spanish conquistadors. When the Spaniards' attempt to conquer the New World failed, they left their horses behind to fend for themselves as they sailed back to Spain.

The horses that survived in the wilderness adapted to the harsh conditions of the area, which was one of extreme temperatures and sparse grazing. Native people used some of the wild horses for food and transportation. The smaller horses were the best survivors since they offered little in the way of usefulness. The larger horses were eaten or put to work, while the small ones were left in the wild and reproduced.

This Falabella, Toyland Macho Chips, was bred by Laurie Stevens of Toyland Miniature Horses and is now owned by Kim Landis of Crayonbox Miniature Horses. He exhibits the Appaloosa coloring favored by Julio Falabella. (Photo by Kim Landis.)

Legend has it that Patrick Newtall discovered small horses that were kept by natives or running wild, depending on which story you are reading, and acquired some of the stock. In the late 1800s he started a breeding program with the small horses, crossing them with the native Criollos and imported Thoroughbreds. What resulted was a very small and refined horse.

Patrick's son-in-law, Juan Falabella, joined the venture, and together they continued to improve the breed. Pony breeds were introduced, the smallest offspring were bred, and finally the Falabella's size was reduced to a standard of less than thirty inches. By the 1940s Emilio and Julio César Falabella acquired the job of record keeping and firmly established the breed called Falabella Miniature Horse. Today the Association of Falabella Breeders keeps the records for all registered Falabellas, tracing their heritage to the pedigrees preserved by those two men.

Foundation Falabella horses were, and still are, bred for more than small size. Quality was of utmost importance along with stamina, presence, and a tractable personality. Their physical characteristics are very consistent throughout the breed, with size averaging about twenty-eight inches. Their conformation is well balanced, with little variation from generation to generation. Their overall appearance is that of a refined stock horse. The most common colors are browns and blacks, but occasionally they crop out with pinto coloring, and some have Appaloosa-type markings. Julio Falabella is said to have favored the spotted horses with pinto or appaloosa coats.

Two horses stand out in the Falabella history. One was Napoleon, a twenty-seven-inch stallion that lived to be forty-two years old. After his death the family erected a monument to his memory on the farm. Many of today's Falabella pedigrees trace to Napoleon.

An Appaloosa spotted stallion named Menelek made history as the foundation stud of Falabella horses in Great Britain. In 1977 Menelek was purchased by Lady Rosamond Fisher and became a resident of Kilverstone Wildlife Park in Thetford, England. His bloodlines are prominent in the pedigrees of Miniature Horses throughout Great Britain and Europe. He unfortunately died after being kicked by a mare.

In 1980 Julio Falabella died, and the herd was divided between his second wife, Maria Luisa, and his daughter, Maria Angelica. Maria Luisa continued the Falabella breeding traditions in South America and exported horses to countries all over the world. Maria Angelica and her business partner, Washington Sea, moved to South Carolina in 1995 and set up a breeding farm there.

Most of the Falabella bloodline found in the United States trace to horses imported into the country by Regina Winery in 1962. Brothers John and Frank Ellena imported twelve stallions to their farm. They decided the horses would be a great promotional tool and used six of them to pull a miniature stagecoach in parades and other public events. The six Falabella stallions had stalls fashioned from wine barrels. By the time the Ellenas died, the herd numbered twenty-two. Norman Fuller bought the horses and continued breeding them.

Falabella Miniature Horses have spread throughout the world, being cherished by royalty and the rich and famous, including Frank Sinatra, Wayne Newton, and Nelson Rockefeller.

REGISTRIES

In the late 1960s Alton Freeman of North Carolina and Rayford Ely, who lived in California, came up with the idea of a registry for midget ponies. In *Moorman Field, Horse Trader*, Jacqueline and Thomas Field credit these two men for changing the name of these little equines to Miniature Horses. Freeman and Ely formed the American Miniature Horse Registry (AMHR), which in 1971 became a division of the American Shetland Pony Club. The AMHR had a thirty-four-inch height limit, and there were nine hundred registered before the books closed in 1973.

Today AMHR horses are registered in two size classifications. Those thirty-four inches and under are registered as Class A; those over thirty-four inches up to thirty-eight inches are Class B. The registry keeps records of pedigrees and competitions.

The American Miniature Horse Association (AMHA) was organized in 1978 in Arlington, Texas, to develop a breed standard separate from other ponies. This encouraged the future of the Miniature through breeding and showing.

The AMHA rules limit the height to thirty-four inches. Foals with registered parents receive temporary papers. If after five years they do not measure over the thirty-four-inch limit the owner may apply for permanent papers. Since 1987 only horses with AMHA-registered parents are accepted into the association. Today AMHA has registered 114,422 horses and in 2003 it had twelve thousand members. There are over forty affiliate AMHA-approved clubs that provide education and comradeship on a more local level for Miniature Horse lovers.

The World Class Miniature Horse Registry (WCMHR) was established in 1995. The books were open to three sizes of Miniature Horses and ponies: Class A for horses thirty-four inches and under, Class B for horses over thirty-four inches and up to thirty-eight inches, and Show Ponies for those over thirty-eight inches up to forty-eight inches. The books were closed in 2004. The registry is headquartered in Vinton, Virginia, and registers Miniatures from all over the world.

The future of Miniature Horses looks bright. It is the fastest growing breed in America. The conformation of the American Miniature has evolved from a shaggy little pony to a small version of two main types: Arabian and quarter horse. No longer does the Miniature slave in the coal mines, nor is it considered an oddity. In addition to being a wonderful pet, the Miniature is found excelling in the show ring, working with disabled children and adults, serving as a guide horse for the visually impaired, and as a premier driving horse. When asked, "What in the world can a Miniature Horse do?" Mini fanciers are likely to answer, "Almost anything."

CHAPTER TWO

PREPARING FOR OWNERSHIP: HOUSING, TRANSPORTATION, AND EQUIPMENT

MOST MINIS ARE HARDY OUTDOORS TYPES. THEY DO NOT require a fancy stable, and fare very well in all kinds of weather with minimal cover. A run-in shed to break the wind and offer shade is the most they need. But, before you start building a shelter, and certainly before you purchase a Miniature Horse, find out if your property is zoned for horses.

While a Miniature Horse can be smaller than a large dog and does not bark, zoning sometimes rules out keeping one in the backyard, or even on several acres. Buying property that previously housed horses, or has a barn and fence on it, does not mean you can continue using it for horses, even tiny ones. Sometimes the original owner operated under a grandfather clause that will not apply to a new owner.

Bess Kelly, owner of Miniature Horses at Bootstrap Manor in Franklin, Virginia, has worked for over twenty years in real estate management. She advises that even out of town you should check zoning before purchase. She cautions to check not only for permission to build, but for any county regulations that control how the property can be used.

"In my area you can have up to three horses on five acres owned, five horses up to ten acres, but over ten acres there is no limit. Plus, [there are] other limits for various animals, as in no hogs and so on. It's always important to find these things out," Kelly said.

A trip to the county commissioner's office or town hall is a must before going to the expense of building a shelter and putting up a fence. Generally, a Miniature Horse falls into the livestock rather than pet category, although some individuals have succeeded in getting officials to change that status to pet. It is also important to know that deed restrictions are not the same as county or city zoning restrictions. Property can be zoned for horses, but the deed restrictions may prohibit outbuildings or limit the number of pets, which would restrict having a Miniature Horse. Finally, always get permissions that are granted in writing and dated, and don't assume anything.

A thick winter coat protects these Minis from the cold.

Once your zoning issues are resolved you can start planning your Miniature Horse's living quarters. A thick winter coat protects the majority of Miniature Horses from the elements when it is cold. Even in the far northern states and Canada, Minis can live outside with no ill effects. As far as the horses are concerned, they are happiest outdoors in any type of weather. Barns are more for human convenience than for the welfare of the animals. Show horses, for instance, are often kept stalled to keep their coats from getting sun bleached, to control their diets, and they are sometimes kept inside, especially at night, to protect them from predators.

The stall door is low enough for a Mini to watch what is going on outside.

Minis do not need as much space as regular horses. An eight-by-eight-foot stall is adequate. The most important consideration in designing a barn or shelter is ventilation. Air movement helps prevent respiratory disease and reduces fly populations. Stall walls and doors are best scaled down to allow air to circulate, and to allow the Mini to look out and see what's going on.

Stables are most commonly built of wood, metal, or concrete block. These materials all have pros and cons depending on location and budget. Normal materials for the roof are tin, shingle, aluminum, or fiberglass. In the South aluminum is a good choice because it reflects the sun's rays and helps keep the barn cool. Aluminum roofing comes in four-foot-wide panels and different lengths and is easy to install.

Pastured horses need a three-sided run-in shed to shield them from the elements and provide shade. A Quonset-style hut is a low-cost and easy-to-construct shelter that is ideal for Minis. The hut is made of two sixteen-by-four-foot-long cattle panels, six T-posts and a twelve-by-sixteen-foot tarp. Drive the T-posts into the ground, three on each side, four feet apart, with 10.5 feet between the two rows. Fasten the two panels together with wire, and then place the ends inside the posts and anchor them with wire at the bottom and sides. The panel forms an arch between the rows of T-posts. Stretch a tarp over the arch and secure it with cord to the panel frame. A second tarp across the back breaks the wind in winter, but can be removed in summer to allow ventilation.

Fences may be a bigger issue than shelter. What big horses can go over, a Mini can go under. Board or post-and-rail fences are a good choice as long as the boards are spaced close enough to prevent escape. It is also the most expensive fence. Some farms use board fence at the front of their property for eye appeal, and use one of the alternative fences for the back of the property. Other advantages to using board for fencing are its visibility and sturdiness. The most common boards used are one-by-six inches. Most fences are five feet tall with a minimum of three, preferably four, boards. Some horses will chew wood fencing, so a hotwire on the inside might be necessary.

A Mini hut provides shelter at a low cost.
(Photo by author.)

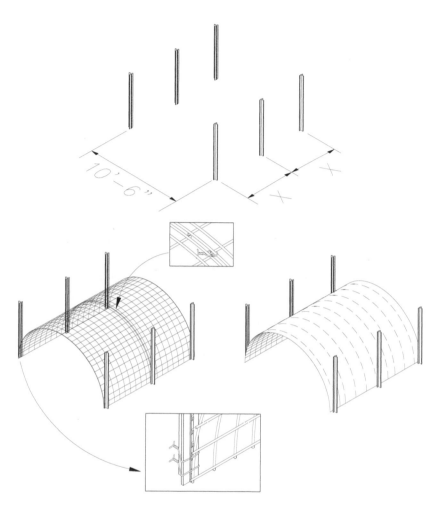

Plans for building a Mini hut.
(Diagram courtesy of Ernest Bradford.)

An electric fence is another good option. T-posts and electric wire or tape are inexpensive, portable, and relatively safe fencing for Miniature Horses. Electric tape is an improvement over wire for two reasons. Tape is easier for the horse to see, so it is less likely the horses will run through, get out, or get tangled in the fence. Second, the tape is better than wire because if the horse does become entangled the tape will not cut into the horse's legs as easily as wire. Most Minis soon learn to respect the electric fence. Two strands placed at twelve and twenty-four inches from the ground and stretched tight between T-posts are adequate.

Wire mesh, called no-climb in some areas, is fine as long as the mesh is small enough to prevent a Miniature Horse from getting a hoof through and becoming tangled. It comes in rolls of fifty or one hundred feet. It can be attached to wooden posts or metal T-posts. It must be stretched very tight to prevent sagging.

Boards must be placed close enough so that the Mini can't squeeze through.

Chain link, two-by-four garden fence, or the new horse fence that is woven into small-triangle mesh, are all suitable materials for Mini fences. A sight board placed at the top will make the fence more visible and add support to a mesh fence. Some Minis like to use a wire fence to scratch, especially during the shed-out season. They will push on the fence, making it sag. A single strand of electric tape or wire added inside the fence will discourage this behavior. Mini owners even go so far as to make a "scratch panel" to satisfy their horses' urge to rub by installing two posts about eight feet apart and hanging a section of hog or cattle panel between the posts. The panels are made of a grid of heavy, welded wire that can withstand the Mini's pushing.

Hog or cattle panels are also economical and sturdy fencing material. The panels come in sixteen-foot lengths and can be nailed to wooden posts or attached to T-posts with wire. Portable welded pipe panels also make very good paddock fencing, but are more expensive. They work best for a small group of Minis. The paddock can be moved from place to place.

Pipe fence panels are portable and safe for Minis.

Fences have to be strong enough to withstand a Mini's urge to scratch.

TACK AND EQUIPMENT

Shopping for a first Mini's gear is like shopping for baby clothes. "Aw, look at that. It's so cute," is the natural response when a customer in a tack shop comes across any piece of equipment designed for the Miniature Horse, whether it is a set of polo wraps, surcingle, or a halter. Fortunately for Mini owners, the breed has become so popular that they can find what they need for their small equines in most tack stores, catalogs, or by shopping online. The serious Miniature Horse person can buy Mini breeding stocks, a scaled-down treadmill for exercising show horses, and strap-on rubber tread shoes to protect the feet of a driving Mini that works on hard-surfaced roads. In addition, grooming tools, farrier tools, and dental instruments come in Mini sizes.

Knowing how to measure a horse so the equipment fits properly will take some of the trial and error out of the shopping experience. For blankets and sheets the horse is measured from the center of the chest, along its side to the tail. The number of inches equals the size, sometimes rounded off to an even number.

All dressed up in their Mini clothes.

As with any horse, good fit is important to the Miniature's well-being. Poorly fitted tack can cause discomfort and sores, which will naturally result in poor performance. Girths and surcingles should be tight enough that they do not slip.

Keeping the equipment clean is also a key factor in preventing harness or saddle sores and it prolongs the usefulness of the tack. Harness, bridles, bits, and training equipment should be wiped off after every use. The leather should be cleaned with saddle soap and then buffed with a leather conditioner periodically. A toothbrush is handy to scrub areas that are very dirty. Soaking the harness or bridle pieces in neatsfoot oil in a plastic bag for a few days will revitalize leather goods that have become dry and brittle.

Scaled-down tack just for Minis.

The metal parts of the tack, including bits, can be cleaned with mild soap and water. They should be rinsed thoroughly to prevent leaving the Mini with a bad taste in its mouth. Brass and silver can be polished with any metal polish.

Horse clothing can be washed in the washing machine using a mild detergent, then line dried and examined for tears that need repair. If the item is weatherproof the mild soap should not hurt it, but spray-on water repellent made for fabrics can be used to refurbish turnout sheets and blankets.

Tack and horse clothing should be stored in a dry room that is dust- and rodent-free. Mice love chewing leather and will tear up blankets to make nesting material, so make the tack room rodent-proof or hire a cat.

TRANSPORTATION

Miniature Horse fanciers have become very ingenious at transporting their small equines. A horse trailer designed for large horses is not always suitable for Minis. The tie rings are too high, and the partition, unless it goes to the floor, leaves room for the Mini to walk under and possibly get caught. To solve this problem some owners redesign their trailers to fit their Minis, or they buy a horse trailer designed especially for Miniature Horses.

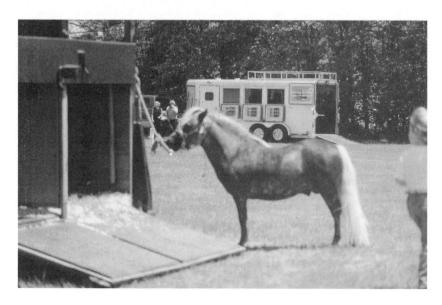

A Mini-sized trailer.

The Miniature Horse Hauler manufactured by Bob Kane is another option growing in popularity with Mini owners. This hauler fits on the bed of a pickup truck, much like a camper. A ramp fits under the hauler and can be pulled out to load the Mini, then slids back under. There is also a cart rack on top of the Horse Hauler. The advantage of this type of hauler is ease of backing, turning, and parking, and no special licenses are required.

Miniature Horses also can be trained to hop right into the family car. Vehicles with high headroom work best so the little horse doesn't bump its head hopping in. SUVs, vans, or station wagons have been commandeered into the Mini-hauling service.

Vans are probably the most popular of vehicles to convert into a Mini hauler. A tarp or plastic floor covering prevents urine from damaging the car's floor. The plastic must be covered with a rubber mat or similar material so the horse doesn't slip. A guard, like the ones made for dogs, can be installed to prevent the Mini from "coming up front." Some owners build a plywood box stall inside the van with partitions so they can carry two Minis.

Converting a cargo trailer by adding windows and air vents can also serve as an adapted trailer for Miniature Horses. While a four-by-eight cargo trailer will be big enough for one Mini, it doesn't provide headroom for the human caretaker to walk the horse in, or for cleaning. When choosing this type of trailer a larger size with more headroom is something to consider.

The 1965 issue of *Look* that carried the story of Smith McCoy's "compact-size ponies" ran a photograph of three Minis riding in the car with their heads outside the window, just like family dogs. Owners who take their Minis for a ride in the car love the funny looks they get when they pull into a gas station or stop for a red light.

Even in a horse trailer footing is a safety factor that should be well thought out. Most people recommend rubber mats with shavings or straw added to absorb moisture. Others worry the bedding will blow around while the trailer is moving and injure the horses' eyes. A fly mask will usually prevent this from happening.

There is a difference of opinion on whether or not to tie the Miniature Horse while it is riding in a trailer. It depends on the horse, how many are traveling, and the type of hauler. Most agree horses do better tied in a trailer, especially if more than one are being transported. One exception is the mare and foal. Many times the foal is not tied so it can nurse and because the baby has not been accustomed to being tied at all.

A slipknot or quick-release snap should be used when tying the horse. The horse needs enough slack to move its head and neck, but the line must be short enough to prevent getting a leg over the rope or otherwise becoming entangled. It is important that the horse cannot jump out if left untied.

Sometimes the horses are calmer if they have some hay to munch while they ride. The hay net must be tied high enough to prevent the Mini from getting a foot caught in the mesh. When hauling a Mini in a car, van, or SUV it is important that it be either tied or a barrier is in place to prevent it from interfering with the driver.

Any trailer being pulled by a vehicle should have brakes, and the vehicle should have a heavy-duty towing package. Most horse trailers require a two-inch ball. The trailer, brakes, lights, and tires should be checked before every trip. The hitch should be checked at every stop.

It is important to take all turns slowly and accelerate and brake slowly so that the horse doesn't lose its balance and fall. When unloading the Miniature Horse the head should be untied first, and if a ramp is used it should be in place before the butt guard is released. The horse should be unloaded in a place that has good footing so the horse does not slip while coming out.

After the Mini is unloaded it should be walked around to restore the blood circulation to its legs before it is stalled. To prevent the floor from rotting, the mats should be pulled out and the floor cleaned thoroughly after every use. Most Miniature Horses are easy to transport when these safety guidelines are met.

CHAPTER THREE

BUYING YOUR FIRST
MINIATURE HORSE

THERE ARE SEVERAL QUESTIONS A POTENTIAL MINIATURE Horse buyer should get the answers to before going out with a checkbook in hand. The most important one is, "What do I want my Mini to do?" Will the horse be a pet or companion, a show horse, a driving horse, or the foundation of a breeding program? Do you want to train the horse yourself, or do you want one that is ready for the show ring?

The next question the buyer should ask is, "What can I afford to spend?" Prices range from hundreds for a pet to thousands for a top breeding or show horse. The more things the horse can do, generally the higher the price.

Novices to horses should take an experienced friend along on their Mini search. Miniatures are no different from other horse breeds in that good conformation enables good performance. The horse should be well balanced, have sound legs, a sloping shoulder, long neck, be clean through the throatlatch, and have a broad forehead. Miniature Horses come in a variety of colors, and are often bred for a particular color or coat pattern, but color should never outweigh good, sound conformation. The ideal Miniature Horse looks like a horse, rather than a pony. Generally there are two types of modern Miniature Horses: quarter horse and Arabian. Breed journals like *Miniature Horse World* (AMHA) and *The Journal* (AMHR) are good resources for learning what type of horses are winning in the shows. These magazines also have advertisements featuring breeding and training farms that specialize in Miniature Horses.

Another factor that determines the price of a horse is age. Young weanlings usually cost less than a mature horse with some training. On the other hand an old horse may be less desirable because of the potential health and soundness problems that go along with old age, and therefore demand a lower purchase price.

Trends can also affect the price of a Miniature Horse. Last year's national champion's color will be the "in" color for the next breeding season. Types, height, and bloodlines also become popular for one reason or another. Trends can drive up the price of a horse and should be avoided, especially if the new horse is not going to be shown.

Good disposition is important in choosing a Mini, particularly if it will be around children. The good news is most Miniature Horses are gentle animals. A horse with a bright ears-up expression is generally a docile one. A buyer should be wary of horses that pin their ears when approached, or threaten to kick, nip, or bite. An experienced horseperson can deal with those vices, but a novice owner may end up with a nasty tempered, if not dangerous, horse. Minis may be little, but they can still inflict pain.

WHERE TO LOOK

The novice can often find a Miniature Horse through networking with friends, the county extension agent, or a veterinarian. The next best method is to buy from a reputable breeder. The parents of the horse can often be seen on the farm, and the breeder may have several horses to choose from. AMHA, WCMHR, and AMHR's Web sites and promotional material have lists of breeds. You can also find them advertised in the breed magazines.

**Mount Airy, North Carolina, auction is the oldest
continuously run Miniature Horse Auction in the world.**
(Photo by author.)

Miniature Horse shows are excellent places to meet breeders and trainers who may have horses to sell. Visit the barn area of the show grounds and talk with exhibitors, look at their horses, and even watch them perform.

Horse auctions are also good places to see a large number of horses at once. Again, caution is necessary. While most auction houses are reputable, an experienced horseman's help might be needed to interpret the auctioneer's jargon.

Two foals rest while waiting their turn on the auction block.
(Photo by author.)

The Miniature Horse auction held in Mount Airy, North Carolina, every spring brings buyers and sellers from all over the United States and Canada. It is the oldest continuously running Mini sale in the world, having begun in the 1980s. Miniature Horse auctions like the one in Mount Airy are held all over the country. At this kind of

Jessica Smith can't resist petting these foals at the Mount Airy auction.
(Photo by author.)

sale the buyer may find a matched driving team, a yearling, pregnant mares, or show-quality geldings. An auction can be an excellent opportunity to observe a wide range of horses, and meet breeders and Miniature Horse lovers from all over the country.

Standing room only at the Mount Airy Miniature Horse Auction.
(Photo by author.)

Miniatures are even sold on Internet auctions. This is probably the riskiest way to buy. A picture doesn't always show the whole horse, so flaws may not be apparent. The buyer should get a contract that guarantees the horse is sound and healthy and able to pass a pre-purchase vet check. The other thing to consider when buying online is the cost of transportation if the horse is far away. In spite of those drawbacks some people who buy horses online are very satisfied with their purchase.

**The auctioneer gives the spectators this mare's
attributes, and the bidding is lively.**
(Photo by author.)

Newspaper and magazine want ads can be another way to find a Miniature Horse. Private owners often post ads in tack shops and feed stores.

Adopting a Miniature Horse from a rescue organization may appeal to some people. Chances Mini Rescue is one organization that works to rehabilitate abused, neglected, or unwanted Minis. Along with many other horse rescue groups, it does great things for horses and helps educate new owners on the responsible care of horses. Anyone considering adoption should realize that these horses often come with special health problems because of their history. Adoptive owners usually go through a trial period in which the horse will be under the scrutiny of the agency before they can have permanent ownership.

However you find your horse, you should examine the registration papers to be sure the horse is registered in the seller's name. If the horse has not been transferred into the present owner's name there may be problems, or at least added expense, getting it transferred. The horse must have proof of a negative Coggins test and should be up to date on its deworming program and vaccinations.

A prepurchase veterinary examination of the horse is always advisable before making a final decision. This does not imply a lack of trust on the buyer's part, it's just good sense. There can be hidden health problems that the seller is not aware of or that the inexperienced buyer won't detect. The buyer will have to pay for the examination, but it can save hundreds or thousands or dollars spent on the wrong horse.

Choose a vet other than the one used by the seller of the horse to avoid conflict of interest. Tell the vet what you plan to do with your horse. There are different degrees of prepurchase exams. A basic exam includes a complete physical and flexion tests to detect lameness. If the horse is going to be a high-level show horse X-rays can rule out joint disease that may cause problems later. If the horse is being bought as breeding stock a reproductive exam should be made.

New Miniature Horse owners are forewarned by more experienced owners that Minis are like potato chips; you can't stop with just one.

Minis are like potato chips; you can't stop with just one.

CHAPTER FOUR

CARE AND HEALTH

IT'S TRUE THAT MINIS DO NOT REQUIRE AS MUCH SPACE AS regular-sized horses, nor do they eat as much. But the little horses do require the same care when it comes to keeping them healthy and well adjusted. In fact novice owners will be surprised to learn that Minis have some unique health issues related, for the most part, to their size.

NUTRITION

One of the aspects of caring for a Mini that endears them to their owners is that they do not "eat like a horse." They require a much smaller volume of food than a larger horse, but the quality of the food must be just as high.

Pasture is the most natural diet for the Miniature Horse. A balance of grass and legume forage is probably all a Mini needs, unless it is in heavy training or is a pregnant or lactating mare. In those cases some concentrates may be added. If quality pasture isn't available, good-quality hay is the next best thing.

Pastures should be mowed regularly to keep them weed-free and palatable. Toxic plants, including cherry trees, nightshade, and jasmine, are often found growing along the fence lines where birds deposit the seeds. Spraying under the fence with weed killer will control weeds. Horses do not like to graze on tall, tough grass. Instead they will tend to overgraze sections where the grass is short and tender. It is important to rotate the Mini in smaller sections of the pasture to prevent overeating and reduce parasite infestation. The pasture can easily be divided into sections with electric tape and T-posts that can be moved from place to place.

High-quality hay will be leafy, green, and have a fresh, sweet odor. Hay must be inspected for mold, weeds, and trash that can cause illness or death. Minis are at higher risk of poisoning because of their small size.

Horses, no matter what their size, need nutrients from six classifications: water, carbohydrates, fats, vitamins, minerals, and protein. The amounts and ratios of these nutrients in the ration depend on the age, condition, and the kind of work required of the horse.

Nutrition—Good-quality hay can meet the nutritional needs of most Minis.

Water

Water is the most important of all the nutrients and is consumed in the largest amount. Proper growth and the working of all bodily functions from hearing and eyesight to metabolism of other nutrients are dependent on water. Horses can only survive two to five days without this important nutrient.

The Mini must have clean, fresh water at all times. The old saying, "you can lead a horse to water, but you can't make him drink," probably came about because horses are picky about drinking water that isn't clean or the ideal temperature—54 to 55 degrees Fahrenheit. At the onset of winter when water temperatures drop, horses tend to drink less and are more prone to colic. Removing ice and changing the water frequently or putting a heater in the trough will be necessary to keep the water drinkable in cold climates. Heaters are available at any livestock supply store and are inexpensive.

Warm weather encourages algae growth, making the water unpalatable and even toxic in some cases. Locating the water trough in a shady area during the summer will keep the water cool. Frequent cleaning and refilling will help control the algae growth and provide fresh water.

The amount of water the Mini will need depends on its diet, amount of exercise, the weather, age and growth, lactation, and mineral consumption. A free-choice salt block will encourage the horse to drink.

Energy

Carbohydrates and fats provide energy for the horse. When the horse consumes more carbohydrates than it needs, it is stored in the body as fat. This is where Minis get into trouble. They are prone to obesity, and obese horses are more likely to founder and have other health problems.

Carbohydrates are found in grains, which most horses will not need if they are fed quality hay or pasture. Horses that are working hard, and not maintaining their weight, may need a supplement of grains. The best rule of thumb for determining the horse's ideal weight is for it to have enough fat to cover its ribs, but not so much fat that you cannot feel its ribs when palpating the side of the horse. All carbohydrates yield the same amount of energy. One pound of corn yields the same as one pound of oats. Fats have 2.25 times more energy than carbohydrates and are also found in grains. Many commercial feeds contain added fat, especially those in pellet form. The fat helps bind the pellets. Fats are less palatable to horses than carbohydrates, but adding a small amount of vegetable oil to the ration can help put weight on a thin horse and also give its coat an extra shine. Miniature Horse owners have learned that supplementing their show horses' diet with black oil sunflower seed, sometimes referred to as BOSS, gives their horses' coat a nice shine; in addition the seeds are more palatable than vegetable oil.

Protein

Proteins are perhaps the most misunderstood of the nutrients. Protein is not stored in the body as fats are; it must be in the diet daily to benefit the horse. The functions of protein are to build tissue, repair worn-out tissue, and to aid in body functions. Protein is circulated through the bloodstream to the cells. If the cell doesn't need the protein for repairs, it uses it for energy; if it doesn't need it for energy, it becomes fat.

Quality protein is most important for young horses, since it is needed for growth. Once the horse is mature the amount and quality of protein is less important. A one-month to one-year-old needs 16 percent to 18 percent protein, a one- to two-year-old needs 14 percent, and a two- to three-year-old needs 12 percent. After its third year a horse will be fine with as little as 5 percent protein in its diet.

While it is true that excess protein turns into fat, it is not the best way to provide the horse with energy; carbohydrates are much better. Some Miniature Horses can have an allergic reaction to proteins and break out in hives. This probably explains why some owners of Miniatures report that their horses cannot eat alfalfa hay. Alfalfa is a legume and is very high in protein.

Vitamins and Minerals

Vitamins and minerals are necessary for tissue growth and repair, to build blood cells, and as regulators for the body. The horse's bone is made up of 36 percent calcium, 17 percent phosphorous, 0.89 percent magnesium, 10 percent fat, and 20 percent protein.

It is important that vitamins and minerals are in the correct proportions in the ration, especially in young horses. For example, a phosphorous deficiency can cause weight loss and a lack of fat absorption. Excessive phosphorous is just as bad as too little. It can cause bighead disease and enlarged joints, also known as hyperparathyroidism. An imbalance of vitamins and minerals can cause horses to develop pica, a disorder that causes the horse to eat inappropriate things such as wood or manure.

Salt is an important mineral that should be freely available at all times for a horse of any age. Salt increases appetite, and in hot weather it helps regulate water consumption.

Horses on quality pasture generally do not need supplements. A mix of grasses and legumes will have all the mentioned nutrients, except water, that the horse needs.

To sum up Miniature Horse nutrition, Dr. Robert Mowrey, extension horse specialist at North Carolina State University, says to feed Minis according to weight, with the same nutritional balance as other horses.

COMMON HEALTH PROBLEMS

Miniature Horses are hardy and adaptable, but can have certain health problems related mostly to their size. They are more likely to founder, develop colic, and suffer ill effects from ingesting toxic weeds or foreign objects than larger breeds. Regular vaccinations against equine disease, deworming, and careful attention to feeding and the environment in which the Mini lives are key points in its health care.

Founder

Founder is an inflammation of the laminae of the foot. These are the tissues between the wall and the coffin bone that hold the foot together. Founder usually affects the front feet, but can be in one or all four. When the laminae are inflamed, the tissue breaks down and "lets go" of the coffin bone, causing it to slip down and put pressure on the sole of the foot. This condition is very painful, causing an increase in respiration and body temperature and muscle tremors. In the most severe cases the bone will penetrate the bottom of the foot, and the horse will usually have to be destroyed.

We have heard stories about ponies that break into the feed room and gorge themselves on grain, sometimes with heartrending results. Overeating is probably the number one cause of founder with Minis, but it can also be caused by concussion, retained placenta in the broodmare, or drinking too much water while overheated. Any time the horse has a high fever, founder can occur.

Signs of founder are heat and pain in the foot. The horse will try to stand without putting weight on the affected feet, or even lie down. The hoof will be warm to the touch. The vet should be called at the first signs of founder, and the horse taken off all food until the doctor arrives. Standing the horse in mud or wrapping the legs in towels or other absorbent material and hosing it to keep it wet until the vet gets there will reduce the heat in the foot.

The veterinarian might treat the horse with laxatives to clean out the digestive tract, and then administer anti-inflammatory drugs and antihistamines. The veterinarian will probably prescribe a special diet and exercise program. Special trimming or even therapeutic shoeing may be required.

Colic

Colic is a general term meaning bellyache. The cause of the belly-ache can be many things, ranging from internal parasites, large- or small-colon impaction, to spoiled food. It is one of the leading causes of death in horses. Miniature Horses may be even more susceptible to colic because of the smallness of their intestines—it takes less to block things up. The Mini's diet should be on the laxative side, grass being the most desirable food, and coarse hays the least desirable.

An interesting cause of colic among Minis is enteroliths, mineralized stones in the intestines that block the small passages. An enterolith forms around a foreign object that was swallowed by the horse, such as wood, metal, plastic, or glass. Foals that chew on their mothers' manes and tails are particularly prone to this problem since the stones can be formed around the ingested hair. The stones develop much the same way as a pearl forms around a grain of sand in an oyster. The small intestines of the Mini are so small that a stone that can be passed through the system of a large horse is often deadly in the little horse. Surgery is the only remedy.

Research has shown that horses with a diet high in phosphorous, which causes a high pH balance in the colon, are most likely to form enteroliths. The incidence of enteroliths can be reduced by cutting back on bran and alfalfa hay, both foods that are high in minerals, and adding one cup of vinegar to the feed daily.

Internal parasites are one of the most common reasons horses colic. It is the easiest problem to prevent with good hygiene and a regular deworming program. Manure should be picked up from paddock areas, and pastures mowed and rotated regularly to reduce parasite infestation. To deworm the Mini an every-eight-week schedule can be followed, or a daily dose of dewormer can be added to the feed. It is advisable to rotate the dewormers using products like pyrantel, bendamidazole, and ivermectin. Even if a daily program is being used, ivermectin should be administered after the first frost in the fall and again in the spring to combat bots.

Narcolepsy

This sleeping disease, not to be confused with sleeping sickness, rarely occurs in horses. Narcolepsy involves a chemical imbalance in the brain cells that control sleep and wakefulness. The subject does come up fairly often on the Internet's Miniature Horse discussion boards, usually in reference to "fainting foals." A survey of Miniature Horse breeders conducted by the University of Wisconsin showed narcolepsy to be a "rare but distinct syndrome in the Miniature Horse."

Narcolepsy is more common in foals, and they do normally outgrow it as they age. The symptoms can vary from a mild muscle weakness to full collapse. The horse may exhibit the condition while being groomed, clipped, bathed, petted, or just while in its stall. Narcolepsy seldom occurs while the horse is being worked. The horse acts as though it has been tranquilized—staggering if asked to move.

The episodes don't last long, maybe up to ten seconds, but there is the danger the horse will injure itself in a fall when it collapses. Narcolepsy can be very frightening to witness. Marnie Schwanke, of Sunset Ridge Miniatures in western Wisconsin, wrote of her experience in a post on L'il Beginnings Miniature Horse Forums (November 12, 2003, www.lilbeginnings.com.forum/):

> *I had a little fainter, last summer. It was my first and scared me; I had not heard of it before. I went out and found her, she was still wet, on her feet, I took hold of her and she fell to the ground, limp. I tried to get her to stand; she was like a little rag in my hands. I laid her on the ground, looked at Nate and told him, 'I don't think she's going to make it.' I really thought she was about dead. Her mom walked over and pawed her, the*

filly jumped up and nursed. I watched her for a few minutes and then took hold of her again to iodine her navel and she collapsed again, just for a minute or two.

Marnie's foal never had another episode and developed into a normal adult Miniature Horse.

A test is available to diagnose narcolepsy, which can be treated with the antidepressant imipramine that suppresses REM sleep. When a Miniature Horse exhibits symptoms of narcolepsy, a veterinarian should be consulted, especially since the symptoms could be caused by a number of other diseases or conditions including EPM (equine protozoal myeloencephalitis) and epileptic seizures.

Hyperlipemia

Miniature Horses and other ponies' systems do not always metabolize fats the same way their larger relatives do. Because of this fact, a condition called hyperlipemia can occur under certain stressful situations that cause them to drastically go off their feed. Putting a Mini on a sudden diet, heavy parasite infestations, pituitary tumors, pregnancy, and lactation can all trigger hyperlipemia.

Instead of converting fat into energy, as happens with most horses when food quantity is reduced, the fat globules in a Mini are released into the bloodstream and accumulate in the liver. This can cause fatal liver and kidney damage. Once hyperlipemia occurs, the prognosis is not good, with only a 50 percent survival rate.

Symptoms of hyperlipemia are refusal to eat, lethargy and weakness, depression, diarrhea, yellowish mucus membranes, and muscle incoordination. The Miniature Horse's diet should be monitored carefully so that the animal does not become obese. Practicing general good health management by having the Mini on a regular deworming schedule and being up to date on its vaccinations are the best defenses against this condition. If a weight reduction diet is necessary, it should be done very gradually and while increasing the

Mini's exercise. When the Mini is being transported a long distance, food and water should be available to prevent sudden weight loss.

Dental

Miniature Horses require regular dental care. They should have their teeth checked every six months until they are two years old, and annually after that.

A horse's teeth wear over time from chewing. The uneven wear causes sharp edges to form on the teeth, making it painful for the horse to eat. The vet uses a special rasp, called a dental float, to file down the sharp edges.

If chewing is painful the horse may swallow without chewing, causing choke or colic. Another sign of problems is "quidding." A quid is a ball of food that is formed and dropped out of the mouth when the horse eats. Bad breath, dropping food, excessive or bloody saliva, swelling, and refusal to eat are also signs of possible dental problems.

Miniature Horses sometimes have an overbite or underbite; their teeth do not mesh properly, causing difficulty in chewing. They may require more frequent floating. Breeders should have the newborn foal's teeth checked by the vet when he makes the first "baby call." After that, the owner should keep a close watch on the foal's teeth development. If its bite is abnormal, a veterinarian should file the uneven surfaces regularly.

By the time the horse is two years old, it will begin to shed its baby teeth. Sometimes the baby teeth, called caps, can get stuck on the permanent teeth. This problem prevents the new tooth from growing through, or in fact can cause it to grow in the opposite direction through the jaw or the nasal cavity. Bumps, known as dental bumps, may appear along the jawline of the horse. Nasty sinus infections, crooked teeth, and severe pain can result. According to Roger W. Kelsey Jr., in his article "Is Your Horse Afraid to Smile?"

Dental—Miniature Horses require regular dental care.

retained dental caps can be the prerequisite to cribbing. The horse tries to get rid of the caps by cribbing, a habit that continues even after the equine dentist removes the caps.

Wolf teeth, the remnants of the roots of a premolar, are located in front of the first molar, and a horse can have up to four. Not all horses have a problem with wolf teeth, but signs such as head tossing, or carrying the head to one side when in the bridle indicate that the wolf teeth may be causing pain. The lower wolf teeth may not grow through the gum, but can still cause pain, like a baby teething. Before training begins, the Miniature Horse's mouth should be examined and any problem wolf teeth removed.

Hoof Care

"No hoof, no horse" is an age-old adage. It has stuck because it is true. Fortunately, Miniature Horses normally have a strong hoof, and with consistent care they are not prone to many problems.

The first step in taking care of hooves is to clean them daily, especially if the horse is stalled or kept in a small paddock. Those tiny little hooves are particularly susceptible to a disease called thrush.

Thrush is caused by an anaerobic bacteria, meaning that the bacteria lives without air. The bacteria is found in the stomach of the horse and is passed through fecal matter, then trapped in the crevices of the hoof when the horse steps in it. The frog, a triangular structure on the bottom of the foot that acts as a shock absorber, should have the consistency of a pencil eraser when it is healthy. It becomes soft when infected with thrush. Other signs of thrush are a black discharge and foul smell in and around the frog. If left untreated, thrush can "eat away" at the bottom of the foot and cause severe lameness. Cleaning the hoof removes the fecal material and exposes the hoof to the air, thus preventing thrush.

Treatment of thrush is fairly simple when caught early. After the farrier trims away the diseased tissue, an antiseptic solution is applied daily until all signs are gone. Keeping the Mini's environment clean and dry helps prevent a reoccurrence.

To the other extreme, a dry environment can also be damaging. The hoof is more likely to crack and chip, and if the frog is dry and hard, it lacks the elasticity to absorb the shock of the leg hitting the ground. Dry, cranked, or hard hooves can be prevented by regularly applying a moisturizing hoof dressing. Another way to ensure the hoof gets some moisture is to wet the ground around the water trough; when the horse comes to drink his feet will absorb some of the moisture.

Miniature Horses can easily be trained to lift their feet to be cleaned and trimmed. Ideally the training starts when they are foals. From the day they are born their legs should be touched from top to bottom and the legs brushed front, back, and sides. Once the foal accepts touching and brushing, the next step is to carefully pick up a hoof without lifting it too high from the ground. Picking up the hooves in the same order every time, that is, front left, hind left, hind right, front right, teaches the horse to be ready to respond quickly. The order doesn't matter as much as consistency.

If the horse is particularly fussy about its feet being handled, a helper should hold its head and say "no" each time the horse moves away from the handler. The helper should stand on the opposite side from where the handler is working and brace himself against the horse's side, acting as a barrier. The neat thing about these little horses is that humans usually outweigh them. It is important to know the leg of a horse is not built to swing out to the side like our arms and legs. If the handler stands too far from the horse and tries to pull the leg toward him, the horse will feel extremely uncomfortable and will pull away.

Regular trimming is essential to good hoof care. Generally, hooves should be trimmed every six to eight weeks. Some Miniature Horse owners who have large herds learn to do this job themselves.

Improperly trimming a horse can cause injury so do-it-yourselfers should first learn the procedure from a qualified instructor.

Most farriers charge the same amount to trim a Mini as a large horse. In fact, it is much harder work because they have to bend over lower to reach the little guys. Some farriers specialize in working with Miniature Horses, which is the ideal scenario.

Miniature Horses are not shod except for therapeutic reasons. It is against the rules for Miniatures to have shoes while being shown. They just do not need shoes, since the Mini's hoof is typically very tough. If kept trimmed and attended to on a regular basis, their hooves seldom chip or crack.

CHAPTER FIVE

MINIS AS PETS

MINIATURE HORSES HAVE BEEN FAVORED AS PETS FOR centuries. Their personalities are precocious, and they make a great match for children and adults. The fact that they are small allows them to fit into family life, and they can be quite happy living in a backyard. Some are even invited into the house for visits.

Not all Mini owners are "horse people." That can sometimes be a problem since a Miniature Horse requires different care from a cat or dog. But with a little research, horse management on a mini scale can be learned, and these small equines can make a wonderful addition to the family.

Rambo, who lives with Tammy Winkel and her husband in North Carolina, is a pet. He's not the first horse to enter Tammy's life, and he wasn't really a planned addition to her family. She already had horses, dogs, and cats.

"He is my special pal," Tammy says about her Mini, "somewhat like a cross between a dog and a horse."

Tammy explains that Rambo follows her around just like a dog when she is working in his pasture. If she stops her work to talk to her neighbor, he nudges her like a toddler pulling at his mama's shirtsleeve, demanding her undivided attention.

Tammy has had other horses, but she thinks Minis are different altogether. She takes Rambo for walks as she does her dogs, and he accompanies her on an evening jog when Tammy feels she needs an extra dose of exercise. Sometimes passersby do a double take, just

Rambo bobs for apples.
(Photo by author.)

to confirm what they are seeing. When they realize it is not a dog, but a horse, they usually stop and say, "Oh, he is soooooo cute!" Tammy says she tries not to let all that admiration go to Rambo's head even though by now folks all know Rambo by name, even if sometimes they forget Tammy's name.

Tammy and Rambo's relationship was not always smooth sailing. They met under less than perfect circumstances. Getting a Miniature Horse was not anything she'd ever considered until one day she saw Rambo in her neighbor's paddock. Thinking it was a Christmas surprise, she admired him from her own yard for several days. She wondered why anyone would want such a tiny horse that was way too small to be ridden. But she had to grant that he was surely a cute little guy.

Curious, she inquired about this small horse and learned her neighbors had found him wandering loose in the road. They caught him before he caused a traffic accident, and started looking for the owner.

The original owner didn't want him back. She said she just couldn't handle him and asked Tammy's neighbor to keep him or find him a home. Somehow Tammy fell in love with this little stallion.

Warned that he had not been handled much, Tammy said, "How hard can it be to work with such a little horse?"

Laughing in retrospect, Tammy said, "Boy did I have a lot to learn about the power and strength of a Mini!" Rambo proved to be a big handful, even with Tammy's previous horse experience.

The vet was called, and Rambo was turned into a gelding. After that, Tammy spent hours just sitting in his stall talking to him, but not before numerous kicks, bites, rears, and a round of body wrestling that gave her a back injury.

Tammy used the round pen to start Rambo's training. When he finally learned what was expected of him she progressed to teaching him to drive. Tammy called on the expertise of a professional trainer who worked with her and Rambo over a period of nine months.

Rambo begs Tammy for a treat.
(Photo by author.)

Rambo and Tammy practiced until they were ready for their first show. Rambo was registered with the World Class Miniature Horse Registry. They entered some classes in the 2003 WCMHR Show in Williamston, North Carolina. Their two years of hard work paid off with a second-place ribbon. Tammy and Rambo have gone on to winning more ribbons in driving and a reserve championship in halter, and Tammy is confident they have more to come.

Best buddies, Tammy and Rambo.
(Photo by author.)

"Having him has been one of the most rewarding experiences I have had, and I would do it all over again without thinking twice about it," Tammy said. "He is now one of my best animal friends."

CHAPTER SIX

MINIS IN SERVICE

BECAUSE OF THEIR SMALL SIZE AND GOOD DISPOSITION, Miniature Horses are ideal therapy pets. Many are used in all kinds of service programs throughout the world. They can easily be taken into nursing homes, schools, and rehabilitation facilities. Some are even being trained as guide animals for the blind.

GUIDE HORSES

Don and Janet Burleson were the first to successfully train a Miniature Horse as a guide horse for the blind. They saw the advantages a horse would have over dogs: the horse has a longer life span, some people love horses and/or are afraid of dogs, and some people are allergic to dogs. Their work has attracted worldwide media attention, and the attention of Alexandra Kurland.

Alex Kurland, who had already made a name for herself in the horse world with clicker training techniques, and her friend Ann Edie, who had been blind since birth, decided to look into guide horses after Ann's guide dog died. They went to visit the Burlesons, and after much soul-searching decided to try training a Miniature Horse for guide work. That was the birth of the Panda Project.

Ann wrote in her essay "The Panda Project: Mission Statement," "The reality of the situation that dogs have such a short life span compared to humans, and that the average guide dog user will need to suffer the loss of several guides during his/her lifetime, became very apparent to me. The thirty-year life span of horses now seemed much more than a trivial advantage to horses over dogs as guides, that is of course if horses could actually do the job."

As a child Ann was not taught to read Braille, use a cane, or function comfortably beyond certain familiar boundaries. She had a hard time coping with other children who found her "different."

Ann always loved working with animals, having had pets as a child. Perhaps she found them more accepting that her human companions. She had also ridden horses as a child and in college. As an adult she continued her riding lessons and became the owner of an Arabian gelding. That is when the seed of the guide horse idea sprouted. She trusted her horse to guide her around the stable, stopping at doorways, and even helping her retrieve dropped items. The only drawback was his size.

It wasn't until she became a guide dog user that she finally felt the freedom of functioning in the world around her.

Ann wrote, "These three threads of my life story—my experience of blindness, my relationship with dogs as companions and working partners and my love of horses and respect for their intelligence and sensitivity—have been woven into a pattern which has sprung to life in the form of the Panda Project."

Their visit to the Burlesons convinced Ann and Alex that Miniature Horses could do the job. The Burlesons didn't have another guide horse ready, so Ann applied for another Seeing Eye dog.

Still, they were intrigued with the idea of a horse, primarily because of the longer life span. The horse would have to be less than twenty-six inches tall. It would be hard to find a Mini that small without dwarf signs. They used the Internet for their search and found a farm in Florida that had a horse the desired size. They flew to Florida to meet "Panda" in person. Grosshill Panda Bear was a twenty-four-inch, nine-month-old black-and-white filly that was beginning a show career in halter classes.

Ann and Panda.
(Photo by Neil Soderstrom from the children's book
Panda: A Guide Horse for Ann by Rosanna Hansen, Boyds Mills Press.)

The training began with Alex using her clicker methods. Panda had to learn to go up and down stairs and accept all kinds of strange places and objects. All of this was okay with Panda. Even getting her used to riding in a car proved easy. She has learned to wait in long lines patiently, let Ann when know when she is being petted, and make sure she leads Ann in the right path, even when the path might be wide enough for Panda's little body, but not for Ann.

"Her bravery is a great asset for guide work," her trainer writes on her Web site, www.theclickercenter.com. Alex says Panda was calm and comfortable inside her house from the beginning. "Nothing bothered her," she said.

The biggest hurdle was toilet training Panda. Alex was able to teach Panda to go on cue when outside, but teaching her not to poop inside the house or car was a little harder. It seemed Panda considered those places her "stall." Panda didn't go when anyone was looking, so it was next to impossible to reward her for going in the right place at the right time. It took the help of a dog trainer friend and watching Panda around the clock to get the idea across. Now Panda is completely housebroken. She rings a bell to let Ann know she has to go.

Panda and Ann attended the 2004 Ohio Equine Affaire for the first time as a working guide team. They had been there before with Alex while in training, but this time they were on their own. Panda worked successfully in the hullabaloo that goes with that sort of event. The bright lights, vendors, horses, dogs, and people who wanted to pet her did not distract her from her very important job. Not even a train rumbling over her head when they were walking under a trestle caused her the least bit of concern.

Ann writes that Panda traveled like a veteran. "She had no difficulty eating or relieving on cue in unfamiliar places. She has shown no fear or defensiveness toward dogs, strangers, or small children approaching and touching her."

In a short period of time Panda achieved a long list of tasks for formal guide work including responding to verbal commands such as "right," "left," "inside," "outside," and "whoa." She will retrieve dropped objects, and judges the safety of street crossings. She stays focused on a task even when faced with distractions like food, other animals, and human attention. That is not to say there are not skills she still needs to improve. At this writing she is in the process of learning to walk up and down narrow, slippery indoor stairs, boarding and riding on public transportation, and negotiating escalators and revolving doors. She is also learning to use "intelligent disobedience" in times when Ann's and her safety are in jeopardy.

Ann is well aware that she and Panda are pioneers in the world of guide horses. She sums her experience with Panda with these words, "The experience of living so intimately with a working Miniature Horse in our human built environment and social world is still such new and uncharted territory that each excursion forms a benchmark for those that follow to match."

THERAPY HORSES

While the guide horses are the most written about and talked about Minis in service, Miniature Horses are improving the quality of life in other ways, too. Maria Pigozzi started HALTER, Inc., in 2001 to help people with special needs. Miniature Horses are part of an animal therapy program that benefits children and adults with mental or physical challenges. Because many of the clients are toddlers, Miniature Horses are less intimidating than a full-size horse or even larger pony. They also take less room and food, which leaves money for other aspects of the program.

Maria says, "The children we serve with multiple problems including CP [cerebral palsy], sensory integration or DNA abnormalities love the Miniature Horses and feel comfortable with their size."

Minis are trained to walk alongside wheelchairs or walkers as the children practice the obstacle course. The participants get a horse to train and show. The Gulf Coast Miniature Horse Club offers classes especially designed for the children.

The taller Minis can be ridden. Maria has learned that thirty minutes of riding is equivalent to three hours of traditional physical therapy.

At-risk teens are another part of the program. The Kids at Risk teens help with such farm work as building fences, mucking stalls, clearing land, and watering the horses. Once they have proven themselves through the grunt work, they are allowed to train the Minis and supervise other teens. Any who don't want to work are expelled from the program. That seems to be the exception rather than the rule. Many remain in the program even after their court-designated time is up.

HALTER, Inc., also runs an outreach program in which the Minis are taken to such organizations as hospices, nursing homes, schools, and community events.

MERCY

The Delta Society of Washington State has certified Miniature Horses as therapy pets along with other animals. One of those horses is Mercy, owned by Denise Pullis. Mercy is ten years old and registered with the American Miniature Horse Registry and the Pinto Horse Association. Mercy is also an inductee of the 2002 AMHR Performance Hall of Fame in Halter Obstacle.

Before Denise got a horse trailer, Mercy learned to hop into the backseat of the car just like a big dog. Mercy visits schools, nursing homes, group homes, day camps, open house for the local ambulance corps, and libraries. She has also gone to lunch with kids who have cancer.

"Folks look at me like I am a few sandwiches short of a picnic when I tell them what Mercy and I do," says Denise, but those who have benefited from Mercy's work think they are just fine. Mercy has even handed her talents down to her babies: two of her four foals are permanent residents of day care facilities in Massachusetts where they are part of the curriculum.

"We normally take Mercy's foals with her when she does her work as the foals learn a valuable lesson in exposure," Denise explains. The nursing home residents and day care children anxiously await Mercy's newest additions.

Mercy goes into the rooms of residents who are too sick to join the group. Denise remembers one incident involving a woman who was celebrating her birthday with her family. She had been a horsewoman in her younger days. Mercy nuzzled her outreached, trembling hand. Denise says, "I saw the light came back into the woman's eyes as Mercy worked her magic."

One assisted living facility Mercy visits has four hundred residents, and Mercy visits every one. When she has to go out for a "potty break" Denise says Mercy lets her know by clamping her tail down and swishing it. Mercy proceeds to wiggle her whole body while swishing the tail if Denise doesn't get the hint right away.

Mercy is trick trained. She can answer yes and no to Denise's questions and can shake hands, bow, and give out kisses. "Despite all we have accomplished, I feel we are just scratching the surface of what our horses can do," Denise says.

The good that a Miniature Horse in service does can be physical as in HALTER, Inc., or social and mental as in the Delta Society programs. Whether the Mini simply entertains a class of elementary students or brings a sense of empathy and acceptance to a senior citizen in a nursing home, the benefits are many. The old saying, "there is nothing so good for the inside of a man as the outside of a horse," is true even when the horse is very small.

CHAPTER SEVEN

SHOWING THE
MINIATURE HORSE

SHOWING THE MINIATURE HORSE IS NOT ONLY DONE FOR the fun of it, but also to promote the breed. While only a few Minis are big enough to ride, and then only by small children, there are many ways to show them in hand. In addition to conformation and color classes they are shown over fences, through obstacle courses, in liberty, and in driving classes. All three of the major American Miniature Horse registries sponsor shows, and there are Mini classes at open horse shows all across the country.

GROOMING FOR SHOW

Most Minis sport a fuzzy coat, especially in winter and early spring. Somewhere under all that hair is a beautiful Miniature Horse. To find that beauty requires a complete body clip. While it might seem like an impossible task, a few tips offered by the experienced will help make the job a little easier. The most important tool is a set of quality clippers with sharp blades.

Before the clipping starts the Mini should be given a bath using a mild shampoo or soap. It might even take two baths to get rid of all the winter grime that can and will dull the clipper blades and slow down the job. After the bath, spraying the Mini's coat with a hair polish like Show Sheen will make the clipping go smoother and pre-serve the blades. It is also a good idea to start clipping while the hair is still damp from the bath to prevent loose hair from blowing all over the place.

Laura Lavallee, owner and trainer at Show-M-Off Farm in Thorndike, Massachusetts, offers tips on grooming the Miniature Horse for a show.

"A dirty horse gives the impression that the exhibitor doesn't care," Lavallee says. "Bathing your horse is fundamental to grooming for the show. Most horses learn to appreciate a bath, especially in the summer heat. It is very important to rinse all of the soap away, or the skin will become irritated and itchy. There are many different shampoos and conditioners on the market for horses. You will see products with color enhancers, sunscreens, and vitamins and proteins. All work just fine, and many grooms use mild dishwashing soap like Ivory or Dove. Again, experiment and find what best meets your needs."

Clip against the grain, or the way the hair grows. Practice makes perfect, but practice on a horse not destined for a show. Clip in long, even strokes from the bottom up, saving the back until last. That is because the back usually is the dirtiest part, and clipping that last will save wear and tear on the clipper blades. Clipping should be done a week ahead of time to give mistakes time to grow out.

The day before the show, the face and the legs should be touched up one more time. The morning of the show re-clip the muzzle to get rid of any whiskers.

Clipping the eyelashes is often done to make the eyes look larger. It is important to remember the horse has no protection to keep debris out of its eyes without his eyelashes. Because of that a growing number of Mini owners consider this practice inhumane and do not do it. A fly mask will help protect the horse's eyes.

Lavallee also advises to keep the tail shortened to the horse's fetlocks. She says, "A long tail becomes a safety hazard to the horse if it's dragging on the ground and the horse needs to be corrected; he will undoubtedly step on it and pull the hairs out or even rear up and over."

This Mini is being officially measured at the show.

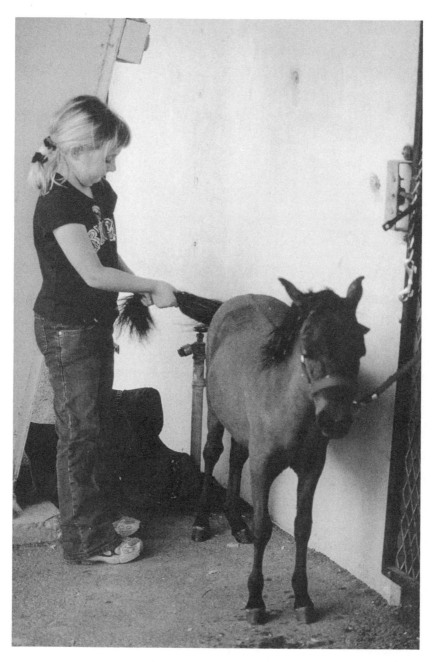

Shampoo and set? A Mini gets the full beauty treatment before a show.

Miniature Horses that are allowed to be outdoors are harder to keep looking show ready. Bleached hair is one reason many trainers do not let their show horses out during the day. However, it is still possible that the manes and tails, especially if they are black, will have lighter-colored hairs. The rules allow dyeing the mane and tail only if it enhances their natural color, but changing the color is not legal. With many products on the market that do the job, including hair dyes for humans, experiment to see what works best for your horse. Most Mini owners prefer the same permanent coloring products made for human hair. Do not use black dye, even for a black mane and tail. It will not look natural, and some dyes even have a blue or violet tint. A better choice is medium or dark brown.

Somewhere under all this fuzz is a Miniature Horse.

Natalie Johnson, of Mount Airy, North Carolina, says a black marker is the secret grooming weapon in her tote box. She uses it to touch up everything from black muzzles to blacking in a missed spot on a hoof. She even uses it to cover a scrape or scab on her black horses.

While all of these tips will help you turn out a meticulously groomed show horse, Lavallee agrees with many other trainers: "Bloom comes from within." Nutrition is the key to a healthy, shiny coat. A balanced diet, exercise, and a supplement to add oils to the skin and hair will do the job much better than anything bought in a bottle.

CONDITIONING

All the experts agree that conditioning starts with good nutrition. Every horse is an individual and needs to be fed according to its individual needs. One of the first things the showman wants is a shiny, healthy coat. There are several ways to achieve this through feeding. The primary way is to add fat to the diet through oils, black oil sunflower seeds, flax seed, or other high-fat foods.

Good-quality hay, supplemented with concentrates, and fed according to weight rounds out the show horse's diet. Many show Minis are not let out to pasture because the sun dries and bleaches their coats, so the hay is very important for these horses. Good roughage is necessary for proper digestion and water absorption.

Exercise is the second part of the conditioning process, especially true for horses that are kept inside during show season. This can be accomplished by longeing, free longeing, and driving. Twenty to thirty minutes is the average recommended time for exercise.

Miniature Horses also need time to play every day for their mental health. Natalie Johnson turns her show horses out every day that weather permits so they can horse around with some buddies. "Playing helps their condition . . . also keeps them happy," she says.

Conditioning the horse to the show environment is also a key point, especially for the young horse. They must be socialized so that being surrounded by people, judge included, will not be stressful. Invite visitors to your barn to pet the horses or just stand close. Enter the stall or paddock as often as possible

IN HAND: HALTER, MODEL, COLOR, AND SHOWMANSHIP

In-hand classes include halter, model, and color classes. There are classes for mares, geldings, and stallions. In AMHR and WCMHR Minis are divided into two size divisions, A (thirty-four inches tall and under) and B (thirty-four inches through thirty-eight inches tall). Further breakdowns are made for different ages: weanlings, yearlings, junior horses (two-year-olds), and senior horses (over two years old).

In a halter class horses are shown in hand at the walk and trot. They are judged for correct conformation, quality, presence, way of going, and type. In addition they must be sound or they will be disqualified, as will horses showing any evidence of inhumane treatment. According to AMHA the breed objective is the smallest possible perfect horse with preference in judging given the smallest horse, all else being equal.

Model classes are judged on conformation only, so the horses are not required to trot. They line up and are judged while posed.

Handlers are not allowed whips, crops, or other artificial aids in halter classes. Children twelve and under may not show stallions.

Specialty halter classes include color classes and group classes including produce-of-dam (offspring of the mare), get-of-sire (offspring of the stallion), mare and foal, and best matched pair.

Because Minis come in all colors, the color classes are popular. Horses are circled (clockwise and counterclockwise) in the ring at a walk; then they are lined up head to tail in the middle of the arena. There are two categories: spotted and solid. In each category mares are shown in separate classes from the stallions and geldings.

Crystal Ridge EK's Image of Fame, halter horse.

Spotted classes were created to show off the varied patterns of pinto and Appaloosa coats. In most shows there are separate classes for pintos and Appaloosas.

The solid-color class includes roans and horses with white markings on their face and legs. In this class the judge looks for a coat with fine texture and a healthy sheen. The horse should be clipped a few days ahead of the show for the coat to grow back enough to give that glossy appearance.

According to WCMHR the judge of the color classes should look for the horse that is most eye-catching in general. Even though according to the rules conformation is not considered (or in the case of AMHR and AMHA only counting 20 percent), it will still play a part in the overall appearance of the winning horse.

A horse that is shown in hand should not be stretched, which means that all four feet must be flat on the ground, and at least one front and one rear cannon bone must be perpendicular to the ground.

The judge takes a closer look.

Laura Lavallee says, "Presentation can make or break a class. Choose your show halter wisely—a thicker noseband can help hide tooth bumps and shorten a long nose, while a thin noseband can create a very elegant appearance on a pretty headed horse."

Exhibitors wait in the lineup for the winner to be announced.

Lavallee recommends that the handler give the horse plenty of length of the lead line so it can move out properly. If you use bait incentive to get your horse's attention, use something you don't normally give to it. For example, she says, "If your horse is out on pasture continuously, then grass probably won't work to get his ears and neck out. Peppermint candies, [wrapped] treats you can scratch, Tic Tacs, and clickers all work well to get their attention."

Handlers should dress appropriately to appear before an audience. The AMHA rules forbid T-shirts, shorts, or open-toed shoes. Long pants or a skirt, a long-sleeved shirt and vest or jacket, and boots are suitable for in-hand classes. Long hair should be worn pulled back or in a bun.

Showmanship is an in-hand class in which the handler's ability to show the horse to its best advantage is judged. The horse's conformation and color are not considered; only its grooming, condition, and the way the handler presents the horse are judged. The AMHA rule book states, "Only the handler is judged. The horse is merely a prop to show the showmanship ability of the youth, but will be considered for appearance."

The class is judged with ten points allotted the appearance of the handler and forty points allotted the appearance of the horse. Those points are divided among conditioning, grooming, trimming, and tack. Fifty points can be gained for the showing of the horse, with leading, posing, poise, alertness, and merits (extra points for answering questions correctly or any additional tests required by the judge).

The handlers must lead the horse in a pattern, which is either taken from the rule book or designed by the judge and posted ahead of time.

When posing the horse for the judge's inspection, it is important that the handler never stand between the judge and the horse because the judge should have a clear view of the Mini at all times. The handler should move from side to side as the judge walks around the horse.

Fifteen-year-old Courtney Pine of Lazy J Farm in Virginia, a blue ribbon winner in showmanship, says there are two ways to do that: the quarter or the half method. In the quarter method you separate the horse into four even sections, two in front and two in back. You can't stand between the horse and the judge, but you should be in a position that allows you to see the judge. When the judge stands at a front quarter, the handler should be on the opposite side. When the judge stands at a hindquarter, the handler is on the same side. In the half method you simply "split" the horse in half, and stay positioned in the opposite side from the judge.

Courtney said, "When you go to switch sides, you always want to do it in one fluid motion. I find standing at an angle to the horse with your toes pointed to the horse makes that task much easier."

She adds, "When you walk to the judge, you always want to make eye contact with him, then look at your horse. Showmanship is all about the way you handle the *horse*. So never let a judge tell you that you didn't look at him or the horse enough. Look at the horse, then the judge, the horse then the judge."

She also warns that when you get to the judge have your horse trained to set up quickly. "If you can't get him to stand perfectly square, get him as close as possible to it, and then look up at the judge (the clue for him to start inspecting). Also, never touch the horse. You will get an automatic DQ [disqualification] for that," she said.

Courtney also gives some tips for teaching the Miniature Horse to pose for the judge.

"I have trained my horse with the commands 'Front Foot Fix' and 'Back Foot Fix.' I just move to the side that I need fixed and tell him that and he brings that foot even with the other. I have worked with him and worked with him on this. Just mainly repetition."

Courtney explains that she uses the lead for different pressures for different feet. To move the front feet she uses light, forward pressure with the lead slightly above his chin, and to move the back feet she uses a bit heavier pressure holding the lead even with his chin. Once his front or back foot is where she needs it she gives the command, "Hold It" before asking him to place the next foot.

The rules require the handler be dressed neatly, and a halter and lead be worn by the horse. The handler's attire includes long pants or a skirt, a long-sleeved shirt, hat, boots, and gloves.

Ideal turnout for showmanship classes.

When asked for recommendations for tack and attire Courtney said, "I personally like western-style halters in showmanship since it is based on quarter horse showmanship and fitting. I always wear a jacket, boots, and belt with belt buckle, gloves, and a hat. Yes, that does sound hot [if the weather is warm], but that is required dress by a lot of the registries and clubs."

The judge can also test the handler's knowledge by asking questions about the horse, particularly the parts of the horse. The handler should be able to answer confidently and quickly.

After completing the pattern and returning to the lineup, the handler must remember she is still showing the horse. The handler must stand to the opposite side of the horse from the judge as he walks down the lineup for a final look at the class.

While in AMHA showmanship is a youth class, there are also adult showmanship classes in the WCMHR shows. It is an ideal class for the new showman to learn how to fit and show Miniature Horses. It is very important to study the rule book of the association governing the show you enter, since there are differences among the organizations.

Both professional and amateur Miniature Horse owners and trainers can find an in-hand class to fit their age or level of experience. Classes are divided into stallion, mare, and gelding divisions, age divisions of horses and of handlers, and there are even entry-level classes at some shows for handlers who have been showing for two years or less.

Once mastering the in-hand classes and watching some of the performance classes owners will no doubt be inspired to show their Miniature Horse in a driving, hunter, jumping, or obstacle course.

DRIVING

Throughout their history Miniature Horses have been trained in harness. In the mines these small, but strong, horses pulled carts, heavy with chunks of coal. They can easily pull a buggy with driver, and sometimes a passenger as well. Therefore, it is no surprise that one of the most popular divisions at a Miniature Horse show is driving. Horses are shown in a variety of ways from single pleasure driving to multiple hitches, and through obstacle courses. Deciding which class is suitable for the horse depends mainly on its way of going. A horse with high action and lots of presence will show best in formal driving, while the more laid-back horse that moves closer to the ground is more likely to excel in country pleasure classes.

Lisa Barnes, of NS Ranch in Texas, has trained Minis to driving championships for sixteen years. When asked what she looks for in a driving horse she said, "It's very easy for me to spot a prospective driving horse. I simply turn the horse loose in a large area and ask the horse to move out freely. A horse with the talent to be a driving horse will have the 'natural' ability to move well. Beyond that I look at the conformation of the horse."

Barnes looks for a horse whose neck comes up and out instead of horizontally for a single driving horse. She also looks for animation, a horse that breaks level at the knee, and how much lift the horse exhibits.

In a country driving Mini, Barnes looks for reach of leg. She likes the leg to come forward beyond the horse's nose. Size is important when it comes down to the judge's decision. Barnes, who is also an AMHA judge, believes the taller Mini has a leg up over the shorter ones.

"However," she said, "there are classes for the thirty-two-inch and under horse, and they too can move and be wonderful driving horses."

According to the American Miniature Horse Association Rulebook, CL-030 Driving General Rules, the horses always enter the ring at a trot. They must be serviceably sound and all driving horses must be at least three years old.

The turnout of the driver and horse is dependent on the class entered. In every case neat and clean go without saying. The rules suggest women wear a dress, tailored suit, skirt, or slacks with blouse, and vest or jacket. A hat, gloves, aprons, and lap robes are optional. Men wear a hat, suit, and tie.

The driver is the only person allowed to handle the reins, and it is against the rules to change drivers in a class. The idea is to give a pleasing appearance while staying within the rules of the class.

Blinders are required in driving classes.

What is not allowed are boots or wraps on the horse's legs, or earplugs. A whip, which is required to be carried in the hand or on the vehicle at all times while driving, should be long enough to reach the horse's shoulder. Blinders and overchecks or sidechecks are also required.

Pleasure driving in a two-wheel easy entry cart.

Several safety rules must also be adhered to. All rules of the road (as in driving a car) must be obeyed, unless officials instruct otherwise, and no horse should ever be left unattended while hooked up to the vehicle. Drivers are allowed to pass another exhibitor, but should return to the rail as soon as possible. If there are too many entries to work safely in the arena at one time, the show manager will divide the class into heats. The top horses in each heat will then be worked, and final placings will be made. Headers, an appropriately attired (show attire or unlettered smock with suitable footwear), capable person thirteen years of age or older, are allowed in the ring at the lineup to stand at the horse's head, and are required in youth classes. The rules state, "The header may not do anything that may affect the horse's performance. Only one header is allowed per horse, may not have a whip and must stay two paces distant from the head of the horse when the judge is inspecting the horse, and at other times unless assistance controlling the horse is needed."

It is important to study the rules before entering a class. They can vary between the different associations. To the novice it may seem all driving classes are pretty much the same, but there are in fact many differences among country pleasure driving, roadster, and formal park driving, the three classes that make up the single pleasure driving division. The judging criteria are different in the order of importance put on the varying aspects of the class. There are also different requirements for the type of vehicle used and the turnout of horse and driver.

Country pleasure driving is judged first on attitude and manners, then performance. After these factors the judge considers the horses' quality and conformation. It is important that the country pleasure horse first and foremost be an easygoing horse that has impeccable manners. The AMHA rules state that high action must be penalized. Instead, the horse should have a relaxed and easy way of going. It will be asked for a walk, pleasure trot, and working trot, which has a longer stride than the pleasure trot, going clockwise and counterclockwise in the ring.

The country pleasure horse is shown in a two-wheel vehicle. A favorite with many drivers is the Meadowbrook, a wooden cart usually made of oak.

The other extreme is the formal park driving horse. This class is for the horse with pizzazz, and the judging criteria are reversed. It is judged first on brilliant performance and presence, quality next, and last, manners and conformation. The formal park horse should exhibit animated gaits, with a walk that is true, cadenced, and collected. The trot should be an extremely animated two-beat cadenced trot with high knee and hock action. The formal park horse carries its head higher than the country pleasure horse, and has a proud look about it. Speed is not desirable at the expense of good form. The vehicles used must be either a fine harness buggy or viceroy.

Country pleasure driving.

The roadster is shown at the trot at three speeds: show jog trot, the road gait, and a full, extended drive-on trot. The horses must not be asked to rein back. The judging criteria call for the horse to demonstrate distinction among these three forms of the trot with smooth transitions, with animation, brilliance, and presence. The roadster should look like a show horse, even though the class is reminiscent of harness racing. The driver must wear colors similar to racing silks, with a cap and jacket that match. The vehicle is a bike, a two-wheeled cart without a basket attached behind the seat.

Meadowbrook Cart is a popular vehicle for country pleasure driving.
(Photo by author.)

MULTIPLE HITCHES

A variety of multiple hitch classes for more than one horse are also offered. There are two main categories: light harness and draft harness.

The horses are judged at the walk and trot both ways of the ring, and are expected to stand quietly, back willingly, and work a figure eight at the trot. The judge wants to see a team that works as a unit. The lead horse should not do all the work. The horses must show excellent performance, quality, and manners, and the horses should match.

Draft hitch horses are shown in a draft wagon or vehicle, and are harnessed in collar and hames. Light harness horses are shown in fine harness with breast collar or full collar (no full hames) and hitched to a carriage or other fine vehicle.

SPEED EVENTS: ROADSTER BARREL RACE AND STAKE RACE

Roadster barrel race and stake race are judged on the speed at which the horses are driven through the prescribed patterns, much like the barrel and stake races in which big horses are ridden. The exhibitors also must complete the pattern exactly as prescribed and maintain a trot throughout the class. Horses must be three years old or older to compete, and they must be hitched to a two-wheel cart without a basket as in the roadster classes. Penalty seconds are added for breaking gait or knocking down a barrel. Entries are disqualified for going off pattern, crossing the start/finish line except at the beginning and end of the pattern, and breaking gait without correcting it immediately. Minor breaks in gait and knocking over a barrel or cone will result in time penalties.

OBSTACLE DRIVING

Obstacle driving is a popular class, and one that most Minis do very well in because of their calm personality. Minis, being the intelligent horses they are, find the obstacle class mentally stimulating and fun.

In an obstacle driving class, the Miniature Horse is driven through a series of obstacles that range from simple patterns marked by cones to backing through or out of an arrangement of poles, cones, or other obstacle. The horse may be asked to go through water, cross a bridge, or stand patiently while the driver picks up an object or gets out of the cart and walks around the horse. The Mini may encounter umbrellas, slickers, or flags that the driver must put on or pick up and carry to another place. The horse must also be schooled in pivoting and backing.

Phillips Domino gets an introduction to harness.
(Photo by author.)

Obstacle horses may be shown in two-wheel or four-wheel vehicles with a basket or floor. Mechanical brakes are not allowed

AMHA classes are judged on performance and way of going, with an emphasis on manners throughout the course. With AMHR classes, however, manners are the main criteria. The horse has sixty seconds for each obstacle, and will be penalized at the judge's discretion for unnecessary delay or excessive time at an object. The horse gets one go at each obstacle and if it misses one it is considered off course and will be eliminated.

Minis are also shown in hand in obstacle classes, which is much like the trail class for regular-sized horses. The rules concerning time allowed per obstacle are the same as in the obstacle driving class.

To prepare for this class the horse needs to be exposed to a variety of objects including things that flap in the wind or sound unusual when walked over. Trainers prepare Minis by leading them in hand through obstacles before attempting to drive them. Hanging plastic bags in the stall or on the fence will help de-spook the horse. Ponying him along on trail rides is another way to accustom the Mini to the world around him and produce a horse with courage and willingness.

Cynthia Tunstall sums up training for the obstacle course in her book *Train Your Own Mini*, "Experience is the best teacher, and exposing your Miniature Horse to all types of situations will help prepare him for the show ring."

Lisa Barnes likes to begin her horses at the end of their second year. She has had older horses come to her for driving training and she has been successful with them. "I prefer that any new horse to driving training come to me with nothing done to them, except to be halter broke and with manners. This way I can go straight to work, teaching the horse my way and I don't have to maybe undo or redo something I don't care for."

This Mini is walking over a series of poles in a trail obstacle class.

Barnes recommends that novices get professional help if they are unsure what to do to avoid problems later down the road. She says sometimes people think just because Minis are little and easy to handle that just anybody can train them. To learn the details of show attire and what's in style, she says to ask around and observe at shows.

Dana Bryan of Dream Weaver Farm in Arkansas has trained numerous AMHR national and reserve champion Minis in driving classes. She says the one thing she looks for in a prospective driving

These legs are made for running.

Play fighting is a fun pastime.

Snow Mini.

9. Most important, do not rush your horse. Teach your horse at its own pace. I know that everyone wants to be in the cart, but your horse will be better off if you wait until it is ready.

HUNTER AND JUMPER CLASSES

Miniature Horses can and do jump beautifully. Of course one doesn't ride them over the fences—they are led in hand around the courses. Other than that one detail, Miniature Horses are shown in jumper and hunter classes under the same rules as their large cousins.

Hunters and jumpers are two distinctly different divisions. In the hunter division the horse's form over the fences, his manners, style, and way of going are judged as he jumps a prescribed course of six to eight jumps. Jumpers, on the other hand, must jump the course with the fewest number of faults to win. The judge scores each jump and totals them. If there is a tie for first place, the jumps are raised and there is a jump-off between the tied horses. It is important to have a copy of the rule book from the association governing the shows you will attend. Each group has some differences in how they proceed. In AMHR shows the jump-offs are timed, with the fastest horse with the least number of faults winning, whereas in the AMHA shows the jump-offs are not timed. Horses must be at least three years old to compete in the hunter or jumping classes.

Training the Mini to jump is very much like training the full-size horse. First the horse should be leading well at a walk and trot, and turning and stopping on cue. Trainers should not begin working the horse over jumps before it is two years old. Even then it is advisable to keep the hurdles under twelve inches until the horse reaches two and a half.

horse is confidence. "It takes a confident horse to move forward while you are behind [it]. A skittish horse that will not leave the herd has a difficult time driving with no one to lead the way."

Bryan says it takes hours and hours and miles and miles in the harness to achieve the collection, form, balance, and unity it takes to win any competition. She listed nine helpful hints to successfully train a Mini to be a winning driving horse.

1. Be calm.

2. Be consistent.

3. Groundwork, groundwork, groundwork!

4. Give lots of verbal praise and instruction while working and driving. Your voice is a direct link to your horse.

5. Use your whip as an extension of your hand to reinforce a command. Example, tap the right shoulder with the whip to confirm that you want a left turn.

6. Don't be afraid to go back to groundwork to refresh your horse or to correct unwanted behavior.

7. Always end your training/driving session on a good note. Even if things have been rough that day, do something that your horse does well and easily. Then give lots of praise.

8. The video camera can be a fantastic tool when training. It allows you to see what is happening with you and your horse firsthand.

Partners in crime.

Mini horseplay.

Show horse.

Making friends.

Enjoying a summer day at the beach.

Blinders are required in driving classes.

Proud Champion, Crystal Ridge EK's Image of Fame.

Miniature Horses are known for their docile dispositions.

You look like a horse, but you don't smell like one.

Give me some sugar.

Mini greetings.

Yee Haw!

Rough and tumble playtime.

Yep, there is a Mini in there someplace.

Just resting.

Look at my long, luxurious hair.

Babysitting.

Sleep is the next best thing to playing.

Miniature horses are shown in jumping and hunter classes.

The horse is usually started over ground poles, or cavaletti. The Miniature Horse is led over the poles, first at a walk, and then the handler jogs along beside it so that it travels across the center of the poles. It is best to have solid wooden poles, so that if the horse bumps it with a foot, it learns to respect the poles. Crossing two poles so they make an X encourages the horse to jump in the center.

When the horse can travel over a series of six to eight poles in an even-paced and free-flowing way, and without hitting any poles, the next step is to raise the poles to about four inches off the ground. At this point the trainer can continue working in this way, gradually raising the poles. The Mini should next be exposed to courses made of a variety of jumps: brush, coop, stonewall, or white fence for hunter courses; triple bars, water, or brush for a jumping class.

Hunters will be required to jump a maximum of twenty-four inches, and in the jumping division the Mini can be asked to jump up to forty-four inches in a jump-off. The handler may go over the jump with the horse in jumping, but it is not permissible to jump over the obstacle with the horse in a hunter class. Doing so is cause for elimination. The horse may go at a trot or canter, but cannot mix the gaits. No baiting is allowed in either class.

The handler gets as much exercise as the horse as she leads it through the jumping course.

Ben Pullis of New York has shown his AMHR mare, Mercy, in hunter youth classes to many championships, including the 2003 High Point Championship for Open Hunter "A" with the Empire State Miniature Horse Association (ESMHA). The duo also won 2003 Reserve High Point Youth Hunter and Youth Jumper for ESMHA and 2003 AMHR Area One Open Hunter "A" Hall of Fame Reserve Champion and achieved their Halter Obstacle Hall of Fame in 2002. Pullis, a junior exhibitor, does his own training. "You have to set up more than one jump, because if you just work over one jump she'll [Mercy] think she only has to go over one jump at the show. So, set up six or seven jumps at home and practice. I reward her with treats when she does it right."

The hunter and jumper classes are fun, and they are good for your health. After all, the handler is running every step of the course along with the horse, which makes for great aerobic exercise.

LIBERTY

One of the most exciting and magical things to witness is a horse running free, mane and tail flying like a crusader's banner. The liberty class is just that. Spectators can watch the Miniature Horse show off in all its glory.

The horse is led into a closed arena, the halter is removed, and for one and one-half minutes it can run free. When the time is up the Mini should obediently return to its handler, who puts the halter back on. No baiting is allowed to get the horse to perform or return to the handler. The handler is allowed to use a whip or noise bottle to encourage the horse to run, but cannot touch the horse in any way with the whip or hands. The Mini's performance is enhanced by musical accompaniment. No outside help is allowed, and can cause the entry to be disqualified.

Judging under AMHA rules is based on style and grace, animation and presence, gaits, music suitability, and the catch.

COSTUME

Everyone loves to dress up, and the cuteness of Miniature Horses makes them a natural for a costume class. The whole family can participate. AMHA has three classes: youth, adult, and group. In the group class any age can exhibit together. The classes are judged on originality and presentation. The horses are shown both ways of the ring at the walk.

Dressed as Florida, the Sunshine State, these youngsters were in the Group Costume Class.

LEADLINE

What could be cuter than a Miniature Horse with a little rider? In the leadline class, children under seven years old show the Minis under saddle while being led by an adult or older youth. The horses are led at a walk in a circle around the judge, and then they line up for final inspection. The Minis should stand quietly and back when asked. Exhibitors should be appropriately dressed depending on whether they are showing with western or English tack. Suitability of rider to horse and the rider's equitation are judged.

Quiet time between classes.

CHAPTER EIGHT

A DAY AT THE RACES— MINI STYLE

MINIATURE HORSES' POPULARITY AS CART HORSES MADE them good candidates for harness racing. Someone somewhere challenged someone else to a friendly race down a dirt path, and Miniature Horse racing was born.

Official pony racing has been around since the middle of the twentieth century. In the 1950s and 1960s, Shetland, Welsh and Hackney ponies were raced, and in 1964 the National Trotting Pony Association (NTPA) was born to organize the various pony racing groups. Today Miniature harness racing is fast becoming a popular sport.

In 1967 pony breeders began crossing their ponies with Standardbreds to boost up the racing ability of the ponies. These pony/Standardbred offspring were called Trottingbreds. Two foundation sires, Lothario and Jade Hanover, are names that show up in about 70 percent of all registered Trottingbred ponies today. In 1977 the NTPA became the International Trotting and Pacing Association, and in 1979 the Trottingbred was officially recognized as a breed.

HARNESSBRED HORSES

James and Arlyn Storey along with Betsy Harms and Arnold Gurley, all who lived in Texas at the time, wanted a small harness horse that young people and senior citizens could enjoy handling and racing. They studied Standardbred bloodlines carefully to give the small horses conformation that would produce added speed. Their mission was to breed for quality; to produce ponies with good dispositions, speed, conformation, heart, and ability. They decided to use Trottingbreds crossed with Minis to reduce size while maintaining Standardbred bloodlines. Some of the favored bloodlines they used were Albatross, Marburg Hanover, Lothario, Florican, and Tar Heel.

Jim Storey and Crystal win at the 1996 National IMTPA Stakes Race in Bryan, Texas.
(Photo courtesy of Arlyn Storey, IMTPA national director at large.)

In February 1994 the first Harnessbred was born. Since that time the breed has risen to over eighty registered Harnessbreds.

Their height ranges from thirty-four to forty inches, stretching the definition of a Mini by several inches. In addition to racing, these horses have the makings of wonderful show horses.

Outstanding Miniature racehorses include Texas Tango, a horse that set the record for the fastest time in the under thirty-four-inch division with a time of 1:18 for one quarter mile in 1994. In the over thirty-four- to thirty-eight-inch category Dancing Warrior took the record with a 1:10 in the same year. Gary Flemming of Florida owned both record-setting horses. Dancing Warrior's record stood until 1999 when Country Crystal, owned by Jim and Arlyn Storey, ran the quarter mile in 1:08. Tross Rojo, also owned by the Storeys, took the record for a 1:03. Rojo is the great-great-grandson of the famous Standardbred Albatross. Rojo went into the midsize category as he measured a little more than one-eighth inch over thirty-eight inches. Both horses' records still stand at this writing.

Today's International Miniature Trotting and Pacing Association (IMTPA) was formed in 1992 to promote the sport of Miniature Horse racing. The IMTPA registers Miniature racehorses in three groups: thirty-four inches and under, over thirty-four inches to thirty-eight inches, and over thirty-eight inches up to forty-six inches. The first IMTPA National Stakes Race was held in 1995 at Bo-Best Miniature Raceway in Reddick, Florida, with twelve hundred spectators and a $10,000 purse in cash and prizes.

In addition to the size divisions, Miniature Horses are raced in time bars. In each racing season there are two qualifying races. The horse's second-best time determines its qualifying time. Each season a horse registered and applying to race receives a certificate of eligibility, which must be renewed by January 1. The horse's qualifying time is recorded on the certificate. This time remains on the sheet until it has to be put in a lower or higher time bar.

To prevent "sandbagging," or cheating by holding back a horse from running its fastest to compete in a slower time bracket, there is the three-second rule. If a horse goes over its qualifying time, the horse's win is recorded, but it does not receive the purse money. The second time it goes over its qualifying time it does not receive the win and has to automatically go into the next fastest time bar. If a horse races under three seconds of its qualifying time for two races, the owner can file a request with the race secretary to place the horse in a lower time bar.

IMTPA maintains pedigree records, race times, track records, and international performance ratings. It also enforces the rules and has the power to suspend anyone not adhering to them. All horses entering an IMTPA race must be registered with IMTPA, AMHA, or AMHR. There have been sanctioned Miniature races in Reddick, Florida; Mount Airy, North Carolina; Lexington, Kentucky; Bryon, Texas; and Buckfield, Maine.

FAMILY FUN

Miniature Horse racing is designed to be fun for the whole family, with anyone from youngsters to oldsters at the reins. Children aged eight to fifteen can participate in the youth division. When drivers are sixteen they race as adults. It is not unusual for owners to train and drive their own horses. The small-sized ponies are much less intimidating for the amateur to race than their full-sized cousins.

Rika Sutphin of Whispering Hill Farm started her relationship with Minis through racing in Mount Airy, North Carolina. Sutphin describes a day at the races as one of family fun that started with a brief meeting, adults and kids assembling separately. The youths would plan a half-time event like a water balloon toss or limbo contest. They often picked kids from the spectators to compete with kids who were racing so everyone got in on the activities.

On a Sunday afternoon eight races were run, four adult and four youth. The announcer called the races and encouraged the spectators to cheer for their favorite. The starter judge made sure all the horses were together at the starting line. On the signal, the Miniature racehorses trotted the quarter mile. If a horse broke into a canter too many times it could be disqualified; the rules were a bit fuzzy in the early days.

Sutphin had a horse that set the Mount Airy track record with a 1:15. She also remembers losing to a horse that broke into a run that lasted the whole race. The judges deemed it technically only one break, so Sutphin's horse lost the race. That was before a protest rule was implemented. "I would have protested the race," she said, "it cost me my [award] jacket for the year. But, that was a long time ago."

The Mount Airy group held an annual banquet to give awards and sometimes raffled a Miniature to pay for the awards.

MODERN MINI RACING

The rules governed by the IMTPA are well in place today to prevent situations like Sutphin's. Two breaks result in a setback of at least one place, as does breaking gait across the finish line or out of the gate.

Miniature Horses are raced on a limited basis of two races for two-year-olds, and unlimited races once they are three. The oval track can be either a quarter mile, or an eighth mile, in which case the horses run two rounds. Like their larger Standardbred counterparts, the Harnessbreds may be trotters or pacers.

The Harnnessbred Breeders Affiliation (HBA) has seventy-two members and has set up training guidelines. It is not at all unusual for Miniature racehorses to also be seen in the show ring winning halter, showmanship, and roadster and driving classes.

Racing adds a new dimension to Miniature Horse breeding. In addition to expanding sales opportunities, race purses are an

Arlyn Storey and Leo.
(Photo courtesy of Arlyn Storey, IMTPA national director at large.)

incentive. The same horses that win on the track are often success-ful in the show ring, especially in the roadster classes. When they meet the height requirements, the Harnessbred can also be accepted into the American Miniature Horse Association and the American Miniature Horse Registry.

Arlyn Storey, who alongside her husband James has been de-scribed as the founder and backbone of modern Miniature Horse racing, says,

The dedication by a few to make Miniatures and mid-size rac-ing a viable sport has been and still is an uphill battle. Most individuals in the small equine industry are in it for showing and driving in the show ring. We, who love [racing], are con-tinuing to prove the physical ability and talent of the small equine by proving them in roadster classes in the show ring and putting on clinics for harness racing. Harnessbreds, the small equine that was developed for Miniature Horse racing, has more than proved themselves with horses like Fort Storey Tross's Rojo, who holds a track record that has yet to be broken, and Fort Storey's Gust of Wind and Fort Storey's Indiana Hustler, first generation Harnessbred stallions in the AMHR Hall of Fame in showing in roadster driving.

CHAPTER NINE

BREEDING THE
MINIATURE HORSE

YOU CAN PICK UP A NEWBORN MINIATURE HORSE AND hold it in your arms. That fact alone can make you want to be a Mini breeder. But, there is a lot you need to know before you buy a mare and a stallion and set up a breeding farm. While the rewards are great, there can also be heartache in raising Minis.

Miniature mares have a higher incidence of reproductive problems than most other breeds of horse, probably because of their smaller size. Therefore, breeders have to be very diligent in caring for their mares' health through good nutrition, deworming, and veterinary care. Owners should keep careful records of breeding and vaccination dates, while any changes in behavior should be noted in writing. It is important to know how long it will take a vet to arrive on the farm so that he can be standing by in case of an emergency.

DYSTOCIA

Because of their small size, Miniature Horse mares often have problems delivering their babies. Many times you just cannot save them no matter how hard you try.

Dystocia means difficult birth. A foal that is too big to fit through the birth canal or a foal turned the wrong way are the two main causes of dystocia. Sometimes the only way to save the mother and

You can hold a baby Mini in your arms.

foal is delivering by C-section. In the best-case scenario the vet can turn a malpositioned foal and assist with a natural birth. Time is all important in any case. If the mare tries too long to pass the foal, the uterus can become prolapsed.

DWARFISM

Dwarfism is another risk that all Miniature Horse breeders take. A dwarf can have any number of defects ranging from minimal to severe. Some of the characteristics are short legs with an oversized head and body, retracted tendons, club feet, an undershot jaw or parrot mouth, a dished face and bulging forehead, and mental retardation. A minimal dwarf usually is one with short legs, poorly aligned jaw, or any physical deformity that does not affect its health. Unfortunately, most dwarfs suffer more severe characteristics. They often require very expensive health care, and do not live out a normal life span.

It is the opinion of some researchers that the dwarf gene exists in almost all American Miniature Horses because in the early days the gene pool was very small and breeders wanted the "smallest horses in the world." Perhaps unknowingly, dwarf Minis were bred in order to downsize the offspring.

While equine researchers have not been able to learn exactly what causes dwarfism in Miniatures, they believe it is most likely caused by a codominate gene. Both parents must carry the gene, but may not always exhibit the physical characteristics of a dwarf. But this gene has not been identified, so there is no way for a breeder to know if the mare and stallion carry the gene except by trial and error.

Dr. Gus Cothran, an equine genetics expert at Kentucky University, gives two reasons why it has been so hard to determine the cause of dwarfism in Minis. One, breeders don't like to admit they have a defect and are reluctant to report their dwarfs. Second, it is very expensive to breed horses for research. There is very little grant money for these studies. Until the demand for research is backed up by money, the cause and remedy of dwarfism will remain a mystery.

He has a lap full of Miniature foals.

BREEDING AND GESTATION

The stallion matures sexually from two to five years of age, although it can impregnate a mare by the end of its first year. While mares are usually fertile by the time they are two, many breeders wait until their third year to breed. The mare has finished growing by then, and the risk of her having problems is lower.

Stallion owners either hand breed or pasture breed. Artificial insemination is not widespread in Miniature Horse breeding because of the small size. Downsized equipment and instruments are not readily available. When opting for pasture breeding, the date the stallion is introduced to the herd should be recorded, and the horses must be observed carefully to be sure the stallion is not being too aggressive with his mares and that the mares are receptive.

Introducing the stallion to a mare.

To be sure of breeding dates and the welfare of the horses, it is better to introduce the stallion to one mare at a time. Hand breeding gives more control over the horses' behavior. This is especially true with maiden mares that may become frightened by the stallion's advances. The breeding records will be more precise with hand breeding.

The gestation period for Minis averages 340 days, a few days less than for average-sized horses. Once the mare is bred, she should receive the same care as any horse for the first eight months of her eleven-month gestation. She should be vaccinated against rhino-pneumonitis in the fifth, seventh, and ninth months and be kept up to date on all her regular vaccinations such as tetanus, sleeping sickness, West Nile, and rabies. A tetanus toxoid shot should be given to the mare the last month of gestation. Mares should be kept under a regular deworming program since parasites are a major health threat to all horses. Not all dewormers are safe for pregnant mares, so reading the labels is a must.

Pregnant mare grazes with herd.

Keeping the mare in good weight is very important. She should not be underweight or obese. The last trimester the mare literally is "eating for two." The baby is growing fast and gets its food from the mare.

To make sure the foal's needs are being met without detriment to the mare, her forage should be gradually reduced and the concentrates increased. Calcium and phosphorus are also important minerals in the mare's diet and the foal's bone development.

Pregnant mares require good nutrition and prenatal care so they can produce healthy babies.

According to "Mare and Foal Nutrition" published by North Carolina's Cooperative Extension Service, the pregnant mare's protein requirements are at least 10.6 percent crude protein to ensure proper fetal growth. The copper content of the mare's diet in late pregnancy directly affects the fetal bone development. Mares in studies that were fed rations deficient in copper had 58 percent more bone and cartilage lesions by the age of three months. Breeders can get help in ensuring that their mares are getting all the nutrients they need from their county livestock agent or from an equine nutritionist.

In addition, it is important that the mare gets plenty of exercise and always has clean, fresh water available. Mares that are out of the barn as much as possible fare better than stalled mares. If the pasture has fescue grass the pregnant mares must be taken off it by the beginning of the last trimester. Most fescue contains a toxic fungus that can cause a long list of problems including abortion, thickened placenta, retained placenta, and low milk production.

"Baby stare" begins the last month of gestation. New owners or breeders with first-time broodmares will want to be available to help if the need arises when the mare goes into labor. Because Miniature Horses are prone to foaling problems, owners should know the signs of labor and keep a close watch on their mares when the time is near.

It is a good idea to gather together some items to make a birthing kit by the last month. Those items include:

- Buckets
- Mild soap
- Disinfectant
- Tail wrap
- Towels
- Ten percent iodine solution and medicine cup
- Enema kit (the child's size)
- Small emergency oxygen tank

The tail wrap keeps the tail out of the way during the birth. Towels are to dry the baby, especially if the weather is chilly. The iodine should be used to disinfect the stump of the umbilical cord. An enema is necessary if the foal does not pass the meconium within twelve hours of birth. The oxygen tank should be used in the event the foal stops breathing. Breeders should know when and how to use it to avoid causing lung damage.

Two or three weeks prior to foaling the mare will slow down her activity. Her large belly will relax and "drop." About one week before parturition the muscles next to the tail head will become very soft. The mare may begin to secrete a clear liquid from her teats a few days before foaling. The secretion becomes thick and has a milky white color by day two. A droplet will dry on the tips of the teats. This is called, "waxing." If edema occurs, which is swelling of the legs, udder, and ventral line under the belly, hand walking the mare can help relieve the pressure.

LABOR

Labor develops in four stages. In the first stage the mare is preparing to give birth. Contractions begin and the horse becomes restless. She may bite at her sides, swish her tail, pace, lie down and get up repeatedly, sweat, and urinate. This stage lasts two to three hours. The water breaks at the end of this stage.

After the expulsion of fluid, stage two begins. As the mare's contractions continue the foal's forefeet and nose appear. This should take about fifteen minutes. If the foal has not appeared within thirty minutes after the water breaks, or does not present front feet and nose first the vet should be called. He or she will have to reposition the foal during this stage. This is not a job for the mare owner unless he or she has training as a breeding or vet technician.

The third stage is the actual birth of the foal. In most cases this stage is uneventful and the mare needs no assistance. If there are no complications the foal will appear within ten minutes after the mare begins the third stage of labor. The membranes from around the foal's nostrils should be removed. If the foal is not breathing on its own the attendant must administer artificial respiration or oxygen. After the foal is born the mare should be allowed to lie quietly so that the nutrients flow from her to the foal through the umbilical cord. If she is left undisturbed, the mare will normally lie still for that amount of time to rest from her labor.

Foals are up and running soon after birth.

After the mare stands and breaks the umbilical cord, the navel cord should be dipped in the iodine solution. Pouring some solution into a medicine cup and dunking the stub is the easiest way to get a good covering of iodine solution. If the mare was not vaccinated with tetanus toxoid thirty days before giving birth, the baby should be given a tetanus antitoxin injection, then a tetanus toxoid at three to five months of age. This is much less effective than the foal receiving passive immunity from the colostrums in the mare's milk. To accomplish passive immunity, the mare must have been vaccinated a month before the foal's birth.

The expulsion of the placenta marks the final stage of labor. This normally happens anytime from fifteen minutes to one hour after the birth of the foal. A retained placenta can result in infection, future infertility, and even death of the mare. If the membranes have not been expelled within six hours, the vet should be called. The placenta should be examined closely to be sure it is intact. Any portions that stay inside the mare can cause infection.

Miniature foals are usually born weighing fifteen to twenty-five pounds and are fifteen inches to twenty-two inches tall. (They reach 90 percent of their adult height by the time they are a year old.) A healthy foal is up and nursing within two hours of birth. It should look bright-eyed and alert. After getting its sea legs, a normal foal will immediately start searching for breakfast. Once it has navigated to the right position, the foal will begin nursing. This first meal is extremely important to the foal's future health. The first milk or colostrum contains antibodies that will protect the foal from disease and contains large amounts of vitamin A. Colostrum also works as a laxative. It is imperative that the foal gets the colostrum in its system within thirty-six hours of birth for it to be effective.

WEANING

A foal of four months old should be getting most of its nutrition from grazing or eating hay and concentrates. It can be weaned without fear of nutritional problems. The weaning experience will go much more easily if two or more foals can be weaned together. If that's not possible, sometimes an older gelding or even a goat can make a good babysitter. They should be kept in a safe environment and far enough from Mama that they cannot see or hear each other. The youngsters and mares should be settled in a week, but that does not mean you can put them back together that soon. Keep them separated at least until the mare quits producing milk.

Come on, Ma, let's play.

Weaning goes more smoothly with a playmate.

Meeting the nutritional needs of the weanling is critical to its becoming a healthy and sound adult horse. The young horse is forming bone and muscle at this stage of life and the ration must be balanced to keep up with this growth. Dr. Bob Mowrey of NCSU in his pamphlet "Mare and Foal Nutrition—Feeding the Weanling and Yearling" recommends that breeders use commercial feed mixes that are already balanced for a specific growth stage. These rations are balanced with the protein, minerals, and vitamins needed. Dr. Mowrey warns in the article, "The practice of adding cheaper, imbalanced whole grains to a balanced mix dilutes the balanced nutrient-to-energy ratio of the concentrate mix. Although the diet may be less expensive, the long-range effect on growth and future soundness could be devastating."

Nap time.

The first year of the Miniature Horse's life sets the stage for its future. How it is fed and nurtured will determine whether or not it grows into a healthy, strong adult. How it is handled will determine how it will behave as an adult. It is an awesome responsibility to bring these new little lives into the world, and can bring an enormous sense of satisfaction and pride, whether the foal grows into a champion show horse, a winning racer, a therapy horse, or a beloved pet.

GLOSSARY

Anaerobic bacteria—Bacteria that lives in an airless environment.

Antihistamine—Drug used to treat allergic reactions.

Anti-inflammatory—A medication used to suppress inflammation.

Artificial insemination—Method of breeding in which the semen is collected from the stallion and injected into the uterus of the mare.

Auction—A sale in which the horse is sold to the highest bidder.

Baby stare—A term referring to the time Mini owners are watching for their mares to have their foal; usually starts the last month of gestation.

Baiting—To offer treats to encourage desired behavior in a horse.

Bighead disease—A condition caused by an imbalance of calcium and phosphorous in the diet. Usually occurs in growing horses, causes limb deformities, lameness, and/or enlarged head.

Bike—Two-wheel vehicle used in racing or roadster classes.

Bots—The larvae stage of the botfly. The fly lays eggs in the horse's hair, the eggs are ingested, and hatch inside the horse. The bots (larvae) attach to the stomach and damage the stomach lining.

Choke—Obstruction in the esophagus blocking the passage of food to the stomach. It can cause death in extreme cases when the esophagus is punctured or tissue dies because the pressure blocks blood supply to a portion of the esophagus.

Coffin bone—The bone inside the hoof.

Coggins test—A blood test used to detect equine infectious anemia.

Colic—Abdominal pain.

Colostrum—A mare's first milk. It contains antibodies that provide immunity against many diseases for the foal.

Concentrate—Food high in energy-producing carbohydrates and fats.

Cribbing—A vice in which the horse sets its teeth on a solid object, arches its neck, and sucks air in big gulps. It can wear down the front teeth.

Criollos—A South American breed descended from Spanish horses brought to the New World by explorers in the 1500s. They are best known as cattle-working horses.

Crop out—A horse that exhibits a characteristic such as pinto or Appaloosa coat patterns or a curly coat when there are no known horses in its pedigree with that characteristic.

Dental bumps—Bumps visible from the exterior of the lower jaw, caused by retained dental caps.

Dental caps—Baby teeth that remain attached after the adult teeth erupt.

Dental float—An instrument used to file sharp edges from the horse's teeth.

Deworm—To administer a medication that kills internal parasites.

Dispersal sale—A sale in which a whole or large part of a herd is being sold.

Dwarf—A small and usually deformed horse. Believed to be caused by a genetic defect.

Dystocia—A difficult birth.

Enterolith—Mineralized stone that is formed in the intestines around a foreign object swallowed by the horse. Similar to the way a pearl forms in an oyster.

Epileptic seizure—A convulsion caused by a brain disorder called epilepsy. The cause is unknown, but believed to be a defect in the development of the brain.

EPM—Equine protozoal myeloencephalitis, an inflammation of the brain and spinal cord caused by a protozoan that is a parasite of the opossum. It is transmitted through fecal matter of the opossum, and can contaminate the feed and water of the horse.

Equitation—The art of riding.

Fainting foal—A foal that collapses under stress, thought to be due to narcolepsy.

Falabella—A breed of Miniature Horse developed in South America by the Falabella family.

Farrier—Person who trims hooves and shoes horses.

Floating—A procedure in which the worn edges of a horse's teeth are filed smooth.

Foundation—The stock first used to establish a breed, and on which the breed standard is based.

Founder—Also known as laminitis, an inflammation of the laminae of the foot.

Free choice—Food or supplements that are available to a horse at all times.

Frog—The triangular shaped part of the foot, that acts as a shock absorber and gives the foot traction. It is located on the bottom of the foot.

Guide horse—A Miniature Horse used to guide people who are sight impaired.

Harnessbred—A breed of Miniature racehorse developed by crossing Trottingbred horses with Miniature Horses to enhance the physical ability of the Miniature Horse for racing.

Harness racing—A horserace between horses that are driven in a bike and harness.

Hyperlipemia—A disorder of fat metabolism in the liver in which fats overload and cause liver failure.

In-hand class—Classes in a horse show where a handler leads the horse.

Intelligent disobedience—The ability to know when to disobey a dangerous command.

Longeing—A method of exercising a horse in which it works on a long lead in a circle around the handler.

Maiden mare—A mare experiencing her first pregnancy.

Meadowbrook—A two-wheel cart used for showing and pleasure driving. The wheels are large and usually made of oak.

Meconium—Fecal matter that forms in the fetus's intestinal track, and should be expelled soon after birth.

Midget pony—The term used for Miniature Horses in the early twentieth century.

Narcolepsy—A malfunction of the part of the brain that controls sleep and wakefulness. The horse falls asleep or loses consciousness, usually under stressful conditions.

Neatsfoot oil—Oil used to condition leather.

Novice—An inexperienced horseperson.

Nutrition—Food and the process in which it is converted to benefit the horse's body tissues.

Panic snap—A snap used to restrain a horse that has a quick-release device.

Parturition—The birth process.

Pit pony—Ponies used to work in mines.

Prepurchase exam—An examination by a veterinarian before purchasing a horse to assure it is healthy and sound.

Paddock—An enclosed turnout area for a horse that allows it room to exercise.

Passive immunity—Temporary immunity provided the foal by the mare through the colostrum.

Pedigree—A record of a horse's lineage.

Picas—An eating disorder in which the horse consumes inappropriate materials like wood, dirt, gravel, manure, or chews manes and tails.

Placenta—The organ that joins the fetus to the mare's uterus.

Ponying—Leading a horse while riding another horse.

Quidding—Rolling food around in the mouth and dropping it because chewing is painful to the horse.

Registration papers—Official document issued for a purebred horse. It shows ownership, date of foaling, and name of breeder. It usually shows the horse's pedigree as well.

Rhinopneumonitis—A virus that affects the respiratory system of the horse. Signs include a fever, snotty nose, congestion, and loss of appetite. It is most serious in young and aged horses. Can cause abortion in pregnant mares.

Run-in shed—An open shelter that a horse can move in and out of at will.

Sandbagging—Deliberately, and illegally, slowing a horse down in a time trial so it will be in a slower division of a harness race.

Service horse—Horses used in various service programs, includes therapeutic riding programs, guide horses for the blind, and pet therapy programs.

Sleeping sickness—Equine encephalomyelitis, a viral infection of the central nervous system.

Slip knot—A quick-release knot used to tie a horse, so that it can be released in an emergency.

Surcingle—Web or leather strap that fits around the horse's girth area, and is used to attach reins for longe line work, or to hold a winter blanket in place.

Tetanus toxoid—Vaccine to protect horses against tetanus bacterium infection.

Time bar—A division in which Miniature Horses are raced, determined by time trials at the beginning of the racing year.

Therapeutic shoeing—Shoeing that corrects malformed hooves, or as treatment for injury or various foot ailments.

Therapy horse—A horse used to teach or help people with physical or mental disabilities.

Thoroughbred—A breed originally developed in England known for its speed and stamina.

Thrush—A disease of the foot caused by anaerobic bacteria. Signs are a thick, black discharge and foul odor. Good hygiene and dry environment are the best deterrents.

Trottingbred—A breed of horse developed by crossing Standardbred horses with Miniature Horses for the purpose of harness racing.

Viceroy—A formal style of a four-wheeled buggy.

Way of going—The way in which a horse moves: gaits, cadence, joint action, and stride are some of the things evaluated in the horse's way of going.

Weanling—A young horse that has been weaned, but not yet reached its first birthday.

West Nile—A virus that causes inflammation of the brain. It is spread to horses and other creatures by mosquito bites and can cause death.

Wolf teeth—Small teeth located in front of the upper premolars.

Yearling—A horse that is one year old.

BIBLIOGRAPHY

BOOKS

Evans, Warren J. *Horses.* San Francisco: W. H. Freeman and Company, 1981.

Field, Jacqueline Coleman, and Thomas Sperry Field. *Moorman Field, Horse Trader.* Fredericksburg, VA: Book Crafters, 1998.

Griffin M. D., James M., and Tom Gore, DVM. *Horse Owners Veterinarian Handbook.* New York: Howell Book House, 1999.

Hansen, Rosanna. *Panda: A Guide Horse for Ann.* Boyds Mills Press, expected 2005.

Tunstall, Cynthia. *Train Your Own Mini.* Zanesville, OH: Small Horse Press, 2001.

Vale, M. M., ed., *The Illustrated Veterinary Encyclopedia for Horsemen.* Tyler, TX: Equine Research, 1975–77.

PAMPHLETS

Mowrey, Dr. Robert. "Mare and Foal Nutrition—Feeding Management of the Broodmare." Raleigh: North Carolina State University, 1993.

——— "Mare and Foal Nutrition—Feeding the Weanling and Yearling." Raleigh: North Carolina State University, 1993.

ARTICLES

"Compact-Size Ponies." *Look.* November 16, 1965, M4.

"Smaller Than a Dog." *Life.* December 22, 1952, 54–56.

WEB PAGES

Boyce, Mary, and Koni Stone. "Hyperlipemia in Miniature Horses." *Stanislaus Journal of Biochemical Reviews.* 1999. www.chem.csutan.edu/chem4400/sijbr/99boyce.htm (accessed 28 August 2004).

Costa, Lais RR MV, MS. "Certain Diseases Affect Miniature Horses." *Equine Health Studies Program Newsletter.* 1999. http://evrp.lsu.edu/v8/8minihorses.asp (accessed 28 August 2004).

Edie, Ann. "The Panda Project: Mission Statement." *The Click That Teaches.* November 2001. www.theclickthatteaches.com/2004/panda/index.php (accessed 28 August 2004).

"Falabella Miniature Horse." *International Museum of the Horse.* 1997–98. www.imh.org/imh/bw/fal.html (accessed 28 August 2004).

Hinz, Harold, PhD. "Possible Causes and Prevention of Equine Entroliths." *Complete Rider.* 1997. www.completerider.com/entroliths.htm (accessed 28 August 2004).

Kelsey, Roger W., Jr. EqD. "Is Your Horse Afraid to Smile?" *Equiworld.* www.equiworld.net/uk/horsecare/dentist/smile.htm (accessed 28 August 2004).

Kurland, Alexandra. "The Panda Project." *The Click That Teaches.* 2001. www.theclickthatteaches.com/2004/panda/index.php (accessed 28 August 2004).

Lamm, Sharon, and Willis Lamm. "Enteroliths." *KBR Horse Health Information, Care and Prevention.* 1997. www.kbrhorse.net/ (accessed 28 August 2004).

McIntyre, Archie. "Pit Pony—When Boys Mined Coal." *Pit Pony.* www.pitpony/movie/whenboysminedcoal/mcintyre.html (accessed 28 August 2004).

Miller, Carolyn. "Millers Equine." *Millers Equine*. 2001–04.
www.millersequine.com/ (accessed 28 August 2004).

Novick, Douglas, DVM. "Narcolepsy—The Sleeping Disease."
Novick, DVM. **www.novick.dvm.com/**
(accessed 28 August 2004).

Ross, Joanne, and Larry Ross. "The Dystocia Dilemma." *Scott Creek*.
www.scottcreek.com/Dystocia.htm
(accessed 28 August 2004).

PERSONAL INTERVIEWS

Alexandra Kurland. Personal Interview. 2004.

Amy Lacy. Personal Interview. 2004.

Ann Edie. Personal Interview. 2004.

Arlyn Storey. Personal Interview. 2004.

Courtney Pine. Personal Interview. 2004.

Dana Bryan. Personal Interview. 2004.

Denise and Ben Pullis. Personal Interview. 2004.

Gus Cothran, PhD. Personal Interview. 2004.

John and Amelia Murray. Personal Interview. 2004.

Laura Lavallee. Personal Interview. 2004.

Lisa Barnes. Personal Interview. 2004.

Maria Pigozzi. Personal Interview. 2004.

Marnie Schwanke. Personal Interview. 2004.

Natalie Johnson. Personal Interview. 2004.

Rika Sutphin. Personal Interview. 2004.

Tamara Winkel. Personal Interview. 2004.

RESOURCES

American Miniature Horse Association
5601 S. Interstate 35W
Alvarado, TX 76009
817-783-5600
www.amha.org

American Miniature Horse Registry
81-B E. Queenswood
Morton, IL 61550
www.shetlandminiature.com

Barefoot Miniature Horses, forums
http://members3.boardhost.com/barefootminisbb

Chances Mini Horse Rescue
418 E. 80 North
Foosland, IL 61845
www.chancesminihorserescue.org/

Falabella Miniature Horse Association
33222 N. Fairfield Road
Round Lake, IL 60073
www.falabellafmha.com

HALTER, Inc.
P.O. Box 5885
Katy, TX 77491-5885
www.halter.us

L'il Beginnings International
www.lilbeginnings.com

Miniature Trotting and Pacing Association, Inc.
18481 Elm Creek Road
Moody, TX 76557
254-853-3744
www.fortstoreyranch.com/imtpa.html

World Class Miniature Horse Registry, Inc.
12009 Stewartsville Rd.
Vinton, VA 24179
540-890-0856
www.wcmhr.com

INDEX